Cultural Policy and Management in Borderlands

This book uncovers the processes at play in the development of cultural policies, projects and networks in spaces at the edge of their countries, marked by their proximity with a borderline.

On a subject which is studied mainly in North America and Western Europe and based on individual case studies, its originality lies in offering a comparative view on the subject, as well as in comparing a European case – the France-Germany borderlands – to a South American case – the Brazil-Uruguay borderlands. Through a multi-sited ethnographic study, the author develops an analysis of the formal and informal processes and networks which sustain this cultural action, looking at the relative contribution of processes led by institutions, cultural agents and the civil society.

This book provides theoretical tools for the analysis of the way cultural ecosystems function in borderlands and is valuable reading for scholars of cultural policy, geography and arts management.

Solène Marié is Head of International Cooperation for Humanities and Social Sciences at France's National Centre for Scientific Research (CNRS) and associate researcher at the Center for Sociological and Political Research in Paris (CRESPPA).

ENCATC Advances in Cultural Management and Policy
Editors: **Richard Maloney**, *New York University, USA, and*
Cristina Ortega Nuere, *3Walks, Spain*

ENCATC has recognised that education in the fields of cultural management and cultural policy cannot and should not be separated from on-the-ground research. Following this stipulation, since its creation, ENCATC has always been very active in pursuing, publishing, presenting and disseminating research in the fields of cultural management and cultural policy to improve and build upon understanding of cultural management and cultural policy issues. In line with the above-mentioned approach, ENCATC established a series of book publications by research award winners and its members.

The series exists to foster critical debate, publish original cultural management and cultural policy research and facilitate discussion about cultural management and cultural policy among researchers, educators, scholars, policymakers and cultural managers. It is also intended to serve as reference material for educators and to support lifelong learning for policymakers and practitioners.

Book Series Publishing Partner
ENCATC European network on cultural management and policy
1, Avenue Maurice
B-1050 Brussels
Belgium
Tel: 0032.2.201.29.12
info@encatc.org; www.encatc.org

Cultural Governance
Current and Future European Perspectives
Edited by Chris Bailey, Elena Theodoulou Charalambous and Geert Drion

Cultural Policy and Management in Borderlands
Creating on the Edge
Solène Marié

For more information about this series, please visit: www.routledge.com/
ENCATC-Advances-in-Cultural-Management-and-Policy/book-series/ENCATC

"Solène Marié builds a remarkable theoretical proposal, contributing to fully understanding political systems at borders, far beyond traditional analyses of cross-border mechanisms. Her very fine understanding of – still scientifically underexplored – Latin American border systems also provides the conceptual bases to a shift in gaze on Europeans cases, notably through her exploration of both formal and informal mechanisms for cultural cooperation."

Anne-Laure Amilhat Szary,
Université Grenoble-Alpes, France

"The jury was impressed by the originality of the topic and its complexity, being conceptually well elaborated and having well-designed research methodology. The comparative perspective and having chosen as the first angle the South American perspective compared to the European one, was highly appreciated by the jury as it was not Eurocentric."

Annick Schramme,
University of Antwerp, Belgium,
and member of the jury for ENCATC's 2021 research
award on cultural policy and cultural management

"In short, excellent, innovative and original work, which enables the understanding of a subject of great importance, putting an emphasis on everyday life integration. A text which deserves to be taken into account by State authorities in the context of public border policies."

Eduardo Palermo,
Centro de Documentación Historica
del Rio de la Plata y Brasil/Universidad
de Montevideo and Museo del Patrimonio
Regional, Rivera, Uruguay

"Her study objectifies precisely the complex arrangements of these borders, and the counterintuitive configurations which they can bring about."

Thomas Brisson,
Université Paris 8, France

This publication was evaluated by the ENCATC Research Award Jury

Jury President
Gerald Lidstone, *ENCATC President, Goldsmiths, University of London, United Kingdom*

Jury Members
Elena Borin, *Link Campus University, Italy*
Dan Green, *H. John Heinz III College of Public Policy and Management at Carnegie Mellon University, United States*
Annika Hampel, *Max Planck Institute for the Study of Crime, Security and Law, Germany*
Michal Lázňovský, *Academy of Performing Arts in Prague, Theatre Faculty, Czech Republic*
Richard Maloney, *New York University, United States*
Jaime Alberto Ruiz Gutiérrez, *Universidad de los Andes at Bogotá Colombia*
Annick Schramme, *University of Antwerp, Belgium/Antwerp Management School, Belgium*
Li-Jung Wang, *Taiwan Association of Cultural Policy Studies (TACPS)*

About ENCATC

ENCATC is the leading European network on cultural management and policy. It is a membership NGO gathering over 100 higher education institutions and cultural organisations in over 40 countries. ENCATC was created in 1992 to encourage the exchange of knowledge, methodologies, experiences, comparative research and regular assessment of the sector's training needs in the broad field of cultural management from a European point of view through a wide range of working groups, projects, activities and events. ENCATC holds the status of an NGO in official partnership with UNESCO and of observer to the Steering Committee for Culture of the Council of Europe, and is co-funded by the Creative Europe programme of the European Union.

About the ENCATC Research Award

The ENCATC Research Award on Cultural Policy and Cultural Management was launched in 2014 by the European network on cultural management and policy, ENCATC, to reward the best recently published PhD thesis presented by a young researcher.

This prestigious recognition aims to stimulate academic research in the field of cultural policy and cultural management with an emphasis on its applied implications. The ENCATC Award also has the ambition to contribute to the process of creating a network of scholars who are competent in doing comparative research projects in cultural policy and cultural management.

The ENCATC Research Award is granted each year to a recently published PhD thesis exploring, through comparative and cross-cultural research, issues at stake and taking a step from evaluative (descriptive) to comparative applied research. In addition, this Award is rewarded to a PhD thesis that can inform policymaking and benefit practitioners active in the broad field of culture.

Series Title by ENCATC Members

N° 7 – Cécile Doustaly (Ed.), Heritage, Cities and Sustainable Development. Interdisciplinary Approaches and International Case Studies, 2019.

Series titles by ENCATC Research Award Winners

N° 8 – Biljana Tanurovska-Kjulavkovski, Modelling Cultural and Art Institutions, 2021.

N° 6 – Alba Zamarbide Urdaniz, Buffers beyond Boundaries. Bridging Theory and Practice in the Management of Historical Territories, 2019.

N° 5 – Rebecca Amsellem, Museums Go International. New Strategies, New Business Models, 2019.

N° 4 – Elena Borin, Public-Private Partnership in the Cultural Sector. A Comparative Analysis of European Models, 2017.

N° 3 – Annika Hampel, Fair Cooperation. A New Paradigm for Cultural Diplomacy and Arts Management, 2017.

N° 2 – Alessia Usai, The Creative City. Cultural Politics and Urban Regeneration between Conservation and Development, 2016.

N° 1 – Elodie Bordat-Chauvin, When Cultural Policies Change. Comparing Mexico and Argentina, 2015.

Cultural Policy and Management in Borderlands
Creating on the Edge

Solène Marié

First published 2024
by Routledge
4 Park Square, Milton Park, Abingdon, Oxon OX14 4RN

and by Routledge
605 Third Avenue, New York, NY 10158

Routledge is an imprint of the Taylor & Francis Group, an informa business

© 2024 Solène Marié

The right of Solène Marié to be identified as author of this work has been asserted in accordance with sections 77 and 78 of the Copyright, Designs and Patents Act 1988.

All rights reserved. No part of this book may be reprinted or reproduced or utilised in any form or by any electronic, mechanical, or other means, now known or hereafter invented, including photocopying and recording, or in any information storage or retrieval system, without permission in writing from the publishers.

Trademark notice: Product or corporate names may be trademarks or registered trademarks, and are used only for identification and explanation without intent to infringe.

British Library Cataloguing-in-Publication Data
A catalogue record for this book is available from the British Library

Library of Congress Cataloging-in-Publication Data
Names: Marié, Solène, author.
Title: Cultural policy and management in borderlands : creating on the edge / Solène Marié.
Description: Abingdon, Oxon ; New York, NY : Routledge, 2024. | Series: ENCATC advances in cultural management and policy | Includes bibliographical references and index.
Identifiers: LCCN 2023051113 (print) | LCCN 2023051114 (ebook) | ISBN 9781032537443 (hardback) | ISBN 9781032537481 (paperback) | ISBN 9781003413400 (ebook)
Subjects: LCSH: Cultural policy. | Borderlands.
Classification: LCC HM621 .M36257 2024 (print) | LCC HM621 (ebook) | DDC 306—dc23/eng/20231117
LC record available at https://lccn.loc.gov/2023051113
LC ebook record available at https://lccn.loc.gov/2023051114

ISBN: 9781032537443 (hbk)
ISBN: 9781032537481 (pbk)
ISBN: 9781003413400 (ebk)

DOI: 10.4324/9781003413400

Typeset in Times New Roman
by codeMantra

Contents

Foreword   *xi*
Preface   *xiii*
Acknowledgements   *xv*
List of acronyms and abbreviations   *xvii*

1 Introduction   1

2 Researching borderlands: shifting the focus   6

3 Cultural production in borderlands: negotiating with the border   28

4 Cultural governance in the Brazil-Uruguay borderlands: policy and activism   40

5 Cultural governance in the France-Germany borderlands: formal and informal dynamics   91

6 Cultural ecosystems in borderlands   105

7 Conclusion   128

Index   *131*

Foreword

At the Centre of the Edge, the title of the thesis which led to this book masterfully summarises the original and innovative undertaking carried out with panache and mastery by Solène Marié. In International Relations studies, in a way, cultural issues and border zones have always appeared as marginal, secondary.

Borders, more often than not, were associated with conflicts and exclusions. Culture and its identity mold in societies were often considered as factors of estrangement and revulsion.

Culture matters. Its dense values, such as individual equality, collective diversity and personal and collective dignity, despite a long history of promoting human rights, still require in-depth and empirically supported studies such as those presented in this book.

Originally, it was a doctoral thesis in International Relations, brilliantly submitted by the author to an international jury of evaluators, from the Universities of Brasília, Montevideo, Grenoble and Paris 8, who enthusiastically approved it.

The book applies pertinent methodological criteria to a topic that requires precision and clarity in the delimitation of its field: the question of frontiers in the study of spaces shaped by human presence and action, as well as the prevalent angles of approach in the contemporary world. The question of the definitions of "borderlands" is very well dealt with, with a background analysis of the contemporary discussion of the concept of "border".

Once the framework of references and concepts is framed, Solène Marié critically reviews the incipient models for the analysis of the themes of culture and border areas, concluding with a thought-provoking and creative proposition of multi-sited ethnography as a tool for the study of everyday international relations.

Two chapters are dedicated to a thorough, original and analytically sound study of specific case studies of the experience of cultural policy and management during the last ten years between Brazil and Uruguay and between France and Germany. This is currently a key issue in the field of International Relations, which has received relatively little attention in specialist literature, which is strongly influenced by a political perspective (foreign policy, systems of government, sovereignty, national autonomy, international organisations, etc.) and, more recently, an ecosystemic perspective (sustainable development, global warming, carbon emissions, etc.).

The book is based on extensive primary sources drawn from field research and interviews. Well grounded in a thorough theoretical analysis of the issues of cultural governance in cross-border regions, the book offers a sharp discussion of the definition of "culture" and of the political and cultural management of exchange initiatives among the partners of the two "twin cities" studied, on the border between Brazil and Uruguay and France and Germany (in this case with a Swiss addition as a contrasting methodical control).

In addition to the wealth of original sources collected during the field study, backed by an analysis of a wide range of specialist literature, Solène Marié has illustrated her arguments with a number of highly original, documented summary tables and images (maps, researched or personally taken photos), which are intended to make the argument clear and immediate. This is an invaluable methodical tool for underpinning her reasoning.

In the context of an international scenario contaminated by ethnocentrisms and the persistent search for regional or world hegemony, the way this book presents its arguments is a new breath of critical independence, thematic innovation, precisely cultural autonomy in no way distorted by any regional or political *parti pris* or adherence to some preferred national standard. On the contrary, as is pointed out in Chapter 6, the book values the windows of opportunity that scientific research and field practice raise.

The many facets of human interaction in life and cultural action collected and organised in the work carried out also represent, in a certain way, a practical action programme for cultural and political operators in international border areas. Perhaps another lesson that can be drawn from this is that culture and the approximation it promotes contribute to a growing awareness of the blurring of lines of separation, transforming them into connecting threads.

Estevão de Rezende Martins
Distinguished Full Professor
University of Brasília

Preface

Cultural Policy and Management in Borderlands: Creating on the Edge uncovers the processes at play in the development of cultural policies, projects and networks in spaces at the edge of their countries, marked by their proximity with a borderline. On a subject which is studied mainly in North America and Western Europe and based on individual case studies, its originality lies in offering a comparative view on the subject, as well as in comparing a European case – the France-Germany borderlands – to a South American case – the Brazil-Uruguay borderlands.

Through a multi-sited ethnographic study, the author develops an analysis of the formal and informal processes and networks which sustain this cultural action, looking at the relative contribution of processes led by institutions, cultural agents and the civil society. She provides theoretical tools for the analysis of the way cultural ecosystems function in the specific spaces which borderlands constitute.

This book is the result of Solène Marié's PhD thesis in International Relations and Political Science entitled "At the centre of the edge: the development of cross-border cultural networks in border cities between Brazil and Uruguay and France and Germany". It was developed at the Universities of Brasília (Brazil) and Paris 8 (France) under the joint supervision of Estevão de Rezende Martins and Thomas Brisson.

This research was made possible by Brazilian public funding. It was carried out with support from the CNPq (Conselho Nacional de Desenvolvimento Científico e Tecnológico) and also received funding from CAPES (Coordenação de Aperfeiçoamento de Pessoal de Nível Superior) and FAP-DF (Fundação de Apoio a Pesquisa do Distrito Federal). In France, it benefitted from the support of the CRESPPA (Center for Sociological and Political Research in Paris, CNRS/Paris 8 University/ Paris Nanterre University).

The thesis received ENCATC's 2021 research award on cultural policy and cultural management, in partnership with the University of Antwerp and its Cultural Management Fund.

Acknowledgements

As Woodrow Wilson admitted in his Speech to the National Press Club (20 March 1914), "I not only use all the brains that I have, but all that I can borrow". This work was not developed in isolation. It could not have existed without the precious and dedicated support of Estevão de Rezende Martins and Thomas Brisson.

I also benefitted from the help of many academics along the way, amongst whom Adriana Dorfman, Anne-Laure Amilhat Szary, Anne-Marie Autissier, Daniel Jatobá, Eduardo Palermo, Elodie Bordat, Fanny Bouquerel, Gutemberg de Vilhena Silva, Guy Saez, Kathleen Staudt, Leonardo Mercher, Lucas Panitz, Rodrigo Pires and Thomas Perrin.

I also had to spend time in the places I studied. For this, I received contacts, information, beds, bikes, cars, food and precious help of all types during my fieldwork. Thank you Glaucia Bernardo, Lia Pachalski, Fernando Damazio, Deisemara Turatti Langoski, Ricardo Almeida, Isabelle, François, Guillaume and Nicolas Keller, Mido, Ana and Gabi Scotti, Hannah and Johann.

To all the borderlanders who accepted to give me an interview, information or some of their time during this research and who live "in the blank white spaces at the edge of the print [...] in the gap between the stories" (Margaret Atwood. The Handmaid's Tale. 1985), I thank you for your trust and your contribution to this work which wouldn't have existed without you.

Finally, thank you to those who are by my side, my family and the friends who helped me in this work: Alina, Ana Carolina, Ana Claudia, André, Caio, Carol, Delphine, Edward, Emmanuel, Larissa, Leandro, Marina, Maurício, Nelson, Roberto and Sara.

Acronyms and abbreviations

ABC	Agência Brasileira de Cooperação
CBR	Cross-Border Region
CETP-UTU	Consejo de Educación Técnico Profesional-Universidad del Trabajo del Uruguay
DRI	Diretoria de Relações Internacionais
ETC	European Territorial Cooperation
EU	European Union
ICT	Information and Communication Technologies
IFSUL	Instituto Federal de Educação, Ciência e Tecnologia Sul-rio-grandense
IPHAE	Instituto do Patrimônio Histórico e Artístico do Estado do Rio Grande do Sul
IPHAN	Instituto do Patrimônio Histórico a Artístico Nacional
IR	International Relations
MEC	Ministério da Educação
MERCOSUR/MERCOSUL	Mercado Común del Sur/Mercado Comum do Sul
MinC	Ministério da Cultura
MRE	Ministério das Relações Exteriores
PAC	Programa de Aceleração do Crescimento
PDFF	Programa de Desenvolvimento da Faixa de Fronteira
RS	Rio Grande do Sul
UNDP	United Nations Development Programme

1 Introduction

Borderlands are frequently considered remote, underdeveloped areas, affected by backwardness and marginalisation (EUROPEAN COMMISSION, 2011). However, as the materialisation of the limit of State political and territorial power, borders are a fundamental issue in the study of domestic and international politics. Paradoxically, it is a minority topic within the field of International Relations, and to a lesser extent in Public Policy and Political Science (PRADO; ESPÓSITO NETO, 2015).

Though bibliographic production on the subject exists, it tends to be produced outside of these core disciplines - mainly within the multidisciplinary field of Border Studies - or to remain within their periphery. This can, to some extent, be described as a form of blindness to an existing debate, which for a number of reasons has not entered the mainstream disciplinary agenda in International Relations.

Within the existing debate on borders, this book focuses specifically on the intersection of the issue of cultural policy and production with that of borderlands, looking at the question of the development of cultural networks in those spaces.

Interest in this issue stems from my past experience living and working in various countries in the sector of cultural policy and production, including cross-border cultural projects. The observed pattern which motivated and triggered my interest was the following: the existence, in some borderlands, of cultural identities and of networks of cultural action that span both sides of an international political dividing line.

The guiding question which structures and motivates the development of this study is the following: How are regional identities sustained in cross-border spaces through cultural production and policy? What is the relative contribution of formal cooperation led by government actors and of informal cooperation led by civil society actors? How does this translate across different cases of cross-border spaces?

Specifically, this question is analysed in the context of two cases of borders that have shifted throughout time, making the corresponding space belong successively to the two neighbouring countries. The first case is the Brazil-Uruguay borderlands; the second is the France-Germany borderlands.

Despite differences between the two cases in terms of relation to conflict and historical process of border constitution, they demonstrate a number of similarities. Firstly, both are characterised by a historical role as buffer space between two regional powers. Secondly, they present a history of successive integration of the area within the two neighbouring states as well as of intense population movements. This confers to the regions under study a specificity in that local history holds the memory of alternating national allegiance. Thirdly, both cases are, amongst Brazilian and French borderlands, those which demonstrate the highest level of porosity between the spaces on both sides of the border as well as a high level of urbanisation and institutionalisation of cross-border processes within their regional context. The Brazil-Uruguay borderlands are the most urbanised amongst Brazil's borderlands, with a degree of urbanisation of 82%[1] (BRASIL, 2009). They are also the most institutionalised, with the largest number of twin cities: six pairs of such cases. Finally, both borderlands present manifestations of hybrid cultural expressions.

On the other hand, the two regions have different levels of institutionalisation of their borderland dynamics: the France-Germany borderlands present a range of public policy instruments supporting the development of the region, from local to supranational level; the Brazil-Uruguay borderlands possess a much more incipient institutional apparatus, especially at supranational level. Whilst cooperation initiatives exist through local and bilateral initiatives, these are incipient at regional level and the Mercosul's involvement is limited to the creation of a favourable environment, with few concrete programmes directed towards cross-border development (CARNEIRO FILHO; LEMOS, 2014).

This book aims to fill a gap in border literature by conducting a cross-regional study of two similar borderlands: one situated in Western Europe and the other situated in South America. Even compared to other regions in the South, the literature on South American borders is scarce. Works focusing on rarely studied or Southern borders include few examples from this region (STAUDT, 2017; ALPER; BRUNET-JAILLY, 2008). This justifies fully the development of this research which, beyond the fact that it tackles an under-studied borderland, includes it in a cross-regional analysis. As pointed out by Newman and Paasi, it is important that border narratives emerge from diverse locations and be put in contrast with literature stemming from the study of European borders:

> It is [...] fallacious to suggest that the removal of boundaries, if indeed that is what is happening in western society, is taking place in the same way, or is having the same effect, within other cultural traditions. We require new

and alternative boundary narratives to emerge from those societies that hold different representations of space and social identities. It is important to encourage scholars from these societies to present their own narratives unapologetically, even, and perhaps especially, where such narratives contrast with our own Euro-centred notions of territorial and spatial fixation
(NEWMAN; PAASI, 1998, p. 201)

The main aim of this research is to examine the processes, factors and actors involved in cultural production and policy in cross-border spaces. It incorporates the following sub-aims:

1 To analyse the combination of formal cooperation mechanisms involved in cultural ecosystems in the two studied borderlands;
2 To analyse the role of informal cooperation in cultural ecosystems in borderlands, in those very borderlands;
3 To tackle the lack of border literature produced in the South, about Southern borders;
4 To provide a cross-regional analysis of borderlands to contribute to the incipient literature of this kind.

An inductive, *case-centred* (rather than variable-centred) comparative approach (DELLA PORTA, 2008) was set up, integrating two phases: firstly, a phase aiming to explore each case fully and individually, integrating elements of social and historical experience, and secondly, a phase of data-driven creation of categories and concepts, based both on the directly and indirectly observable elements of each case studied (SCHREIER, 2012), put in relation with broader theory (PAASI, 2011). The aim of this approach is to ensure that each of the cases is seen for what it is and not as an illustration of a pre-established theory (LEANDER, 1997).

The aim of this research, based on accounts which seek to respect the singularity and specificity of each case's trajectory, is to draw interpretation from the confrontation of these two accounts. In order to respect the cultural and historic specificities of each case, the theoretical and inferential claims are thus more modest.

One of the major differences between the two chosen cases is the degree of institutionalisation of cross-border cultural production. This could potentially bring a certain level of bias to the comparison of the cases. The fieldwork was therefore conducted in the Brazil-Uruguay borderlands before the more institutionalised France-Germany borderlands in order to reduce perceptive bias. Subsequently, fieldwork demonstrated clearly the importance of informal institutions, cooperation and networks for the study of our object. Thus, the adopted perspective includes both formal and informal frameworks, in a multi-scale approach.

4   *Introduction*

For each of the cases, an initial field trip was made throughout the borderlands as extensively as possible and focused on observation as a form of contact with the space, issues and people. Subsequently, a second field trip was organised for data collection in a number of locations identified during the previous field trip. After initial contact with a small number of actors in each site, connections and relationships were followed according to the snowball method.

Observation thus took place in the Brazil-Uruguay borderlands in July 2018, followed by data collection in September 2018. It included the collection of archival documents; participant observation in an event bringing together artists and producers from the borderlands; and interviews with public agents involved in cultural policy, local development and international relations at various levels of government, directors of cultural institutions, artists, cultural producers and managers, and university professors.

Observation took place in the France-Germany borderlands in January 2019, followed by data collection in May–June 2019. It included participant observation in two events bringing together cultural managers from the borderlands and European Union cultural programme representatives, and interviews with officials involved in cultural policy at various levels of government (municipal, regional, European Union), producers and cultural managers, artists, members of a cultural policy think tank and university professors.

Due to the strong disparity between the quantity of existing literature and the quality of primary data on the first and second cases, an emphasis was put on the first case (Brazil-Uruguay borderlands) in terms of data collection and existing literature. This study is therefore asymmetrical. This posture stemmed both from the necessity of access to data on the first case (requiring more extensive interviews) and from the risk of perceptive bias due to the existence of a more developed literature on the European cases, which could result in a Eurocentric bias in the approach to the first case. Finally, it resulted from the aim of producing literature on South American borders. The second case, the France-Germany borderlands, is therefore approached here as a shadow case presenting a counterpoint to the first one in order to bring depth and contrast to the analysis.

It is important to note that a common weakness of research on borderlands is the fact that, rather than being truly elaborated from the borderlands, the researcher's perception is rooted in one side of the borderlands. With this in mind, an attempt was made to enter different borderland networks and gather as many viewpoints as possible. However, it is important to acknowledge the fact that, the description and analysis of processes and actors included in this study are more rooted in the Brazilian and French sides of their respective borderlands due to a more in-depth knowledge of these two countries.

Note

1 Data from 2009.

References

ALPER, D.; BRUNET-JAILLY, E. Special issue: 'Rarely studied borderlands'. **Journal of Borderlands Studies**, v. 23, n. 3, pp. 1–5, 2008.
BRASIL. **Cartilha do Programa de Desenvolvimento da Faixa de Fronteira** (PDFF). Brasília, 2009.
CARNEIRO FILHO, C. P.; LEMOS, B. de O. Brasil e Mercosul : Iniciativas de cooperação fronteiriça. **ACTA Geográfica**, special issue pp. 203–219, 2014.
DELLA PORTA, Donatella. Comparative analysis: Case-oriented versus variable-oriented research. In: DELLA PORTA, Donatella; KEATING, Michael (org.). **Approaches and Methodologies in the Social Sciences: A Pluralist Perspective.** Cambridge, New York: Cambridge University Press, pp. 198–222, 2008.
EUROPEAN COMMISSION. **European Territorial Cooperation - Building Bridges Between People.** Brussels, 2011.
LEANDER, Anna. Bertrand Badie: Cultural Diversity Changing International Relations. In NEUMANN, Iver B., WAEVER, Ole [dir.]. **The Future of International Relations. Masters in the Making?.** London: Routledge, pp. 155–181, 1997.
NEWMAN, David; PAASI, Ansi. Fences and Neighbours in the Postmodern world: Boundary Narratives in Political Geography. Progress in Human Geography, v. 22, n. 2, pp. 186–207, 1998.
PAASI, Anssi. A border theory: An unattainable dream or a realistic aim for border scholars? In: WASTL-WALTER, Doris [ed.]. **The Ashgate Research Companion to Border Studies.** Farnham: Ashgate, pp. 11–32, 2011.
PRADO, Henrique Sartori de Almeida; ESPÓSITO NETO, Tomaz [org.]. **Fronteiras e relações internacionais.** Curitiba: Ithala, 2015.
SCHREIER, Margrit. **Qualitative Content Analysis in Practice.** London: Sage, 2012.
STAUDT, Kathleen. **Border Politics in a Global Era.** Lanham: Rowman & Littlefield, 2017.

2 Researching borderlands
Shifting the focus

2.1 What is a border (space)?

Surrealist artist René Magritte's famous painting named *The treachery of images*, which displays a Pipe above the phrase "This is not a pipe", is a very well-known reflection on the themes of representation, images and the world. It plays with the viewer to make a point about the difference between the representation of an object and the object itself.

A similar look can be cast on borders and their representation, as highlighted by Henk Van Houtum (2011, p. 50):

> The reality of the border [...] is created by the meaning that is attached to it. A line in the sand is not always a limit, as well as a border is not always a line in the sand. A line is geometry, a border is interpretation.

Is this a border?

Figure 2.1 Map of the border between Argentina and Brazil
Credit: Laboratório Nacional de Computação Científica. Licensed under CC BY-ND 3.0.

DOI: 10.4324/9781003413400-2

Researching borderlands: shifting the focus 7

Is this a border?

Figure 2.2 Satellite view of the border between Argentina and Brazil
Credit: Google

Is this a border?

Figure 2.3 Street sign marking the border between Brazil and Uruguay
Credit: Solène Marié

Just as Magritte's works aimed to question mimetic conventions in painting, "the task of critically analysing world politics is to make fuller use of various faculties and to challenge the mimetic and exclusive conventions of Realist international politics" (BLEIKER, 2001, p. 515). For this reason, it is important to start our argument with a reflection on the multidimensional nature of borders as objects, as well as on their representation. As evidenced by Alfred Korzybski, "A map *is not* the territory it represents, but, if correct, it has a *similar structure* to the territory, which accounts for its usefulness" (KORZYBSKI, 1933, p. 58). Thus, it needs to be seen for what it is: a representation.

As highlighted by Bleiker (2001, p. 515), "Representation is always an act of power. This power is at its peak if a form of representation is able to disguise its subjective origins and values". Thus, it is of crucial importance to question ourselves not only on the representation of borders but also on the people, organisations and institutions which produce these representations.

2.1.1 Borders as limits: "on the edge" between us and them

Analysing the etymology of the word border in different languages, a number of interpretations can be made. Firstly, in Romance languages, words such as *fronteira* in Portuguese, *frontera* in Spanish or *frontière* in French, but also the word "frontier" in English which has the same origin, can be seen as derived from the word "front". They are thus linked to the idea of conflict for space from a time which preceded the existence of boundaries as linear devices (AMILHAT SZARY, 2015). According to Foucher (2009), the passage from a conflictual relationship to a pacific one in these areas marks the transition from the "front" to the "frontier".

Machado's interpretation of the etymology of the Portuguese word is slightly different: according to her, it refers to "that which is in front" (OSÓRIO MACHADO, 1998, p. 41). In this interpretation, the historical origin of the word isn't legal, political or intellectual. It indicates that the word was born as a fact of spontaneous social life, referring to the edges of the populated world. This vision also transmits the idea of the border as being the place from which the territory can be expanded: in other words, its beginning.

The English words "boundary" and "border" suggest that in this Germanic language, the idea of border is that of an object which binds, thus transmitting the idea of friction between the internal and the external (AMILHAT SZARY, 2015). Similarly, the word *limite* used in French, Portuguese and Spanish to refer to boundaries and which derives from the Latin term limes or limitis originally used to refer to the outside border of the Roman Empire, carries the idea of the end of a unit, of an "inside".

Thus, whilst the word "frontier" brings the idea of an orientation towards an outside (centrifugal movement), the word "limit" refers to the edge of an inside (centripetal movement).

Finally, the German word *grenze* has its origins in a Polish word meaning "milestone" which refers to the demarcation of private property (AMILHAT SZARY, 2015). Thus, it has a closer relation to territory and its inhabitants.

Table 2.1 summarises the various origins and interpretations of each word.

Table 2.1 Terms used to refer to borders, their etymology and interpretations

Term	Etymology	Interpretation
Border/Boundary (Eng)	An object which binds	Division between an internal and an external
Frontière (Fr) *Fronteira* (Port) *Frontera* (Sp) *Frontier* (Eng)	(1) The front (2) That which is in front	Conflict for territory Relation between two units (in the social and cognitive sense)
Limite (Fr, Port, Esp) *Limit* (Eng)	The end of a unit	Division between an internal and an external
Grenze (Ger)	A milestone	Demarcation of territory

Credit: Solène Marié

Despite variations in etymology and interpretation, these different terms used to refer to borders all carry the idea of a separation between entities, not necessarily related to the existence of a national State. *De facto*, borders have been in existence since the advent of human communities, with the aim of distinguishing an 'us' from a 'them' in order to consolidate human groups' identities (FOUCHER, 1991). Borders are therefore a "social practice of spatial differentiation" (VAN HOUTUM; VAN NAERSSEN, 2002, p. 126) which is inherent to the existence of human groups and has evolved throughout time, but has never disappeared (RAFFESTIN, 1980).

It is with the Peace of Westphalia, a series of treaties (Münster and Osnabrück Treaties) signed in 1648 which put an end to European wars of religion, which the concept gained a political aspect and was associated with the aim of managing territory: it marked the end of the feudal system. With these treaties were created a number of principles which are at the basis of modern international relations, including sovereignty and the inviolability of borders. Borders thus came to be seen as linear and consolidated limits. Correspondingly, the notion of nationality came to be based on the idea of the coherence between a population, a nation and a State (HOBSBAWM, 2000). The resulting political unity was conceived jointly with a cultural unity which could be imposed upon all the members of the given territory. Combined with the principle of sovereignty, borders became marks of a political, social and cultural limit between sovereign States.

Borders, as a consequence of this, are conceived primarily as lines and in a logic of separation. They represent a delimitation between two territories and their appropriation by humans, and consequently, they are analysed based on the prevalent notions of State and sovereignty. They are the physical representation of the separation of territories into sovereign political units, therefore the "physical and static outcome of a political decision-making process" (NEWMAN, 2006, p. 175).

The first scholars who came to conceptualise the notion of border can mostly be found within the discipline of geography, more specifically of geopolitics. Consequently, their work has had a lot of influence on subsequent work on borders within other fields. Rudolf Kjéllen, one of the "founding fathers" of geopolitics, brought forth the idea of States as similar to living beings. Based on this analogy, borders are seen as a living being's skin, enabling the division between the internal and external spaces and constituting the first receptors of information emanating from the external, subsequently communicating them to the "State brain".

This conception of borders can also be found in realist International Relations scholarship. In neorealist approaches, borders represent the separation between an internal order and an external anarchy (WALTZ, 1979) and thus constitute necessary containing barriers against threats coming from the outside.

Borders also constitute limits as a result of discursive practices aimed at making places through an "act of purification, as it is arbitrarily searching for a justifiable, bounded cohesion of people and their activities in space which can be compared and contrasted to other spatial entities" (VAN HOUTUM; VAN NAERSSEN, 2002, p. 126). This separation does not limit itself to space but also to the time of (national) histories, to societies, to languages and to economies: its function is therefore related to representation (FOUCHER, 1991).

Finally, the image of borders as based on geographic features is predominant in the common sense. In practice, a number of borders are based on natural barriers such as rivers, mountains or forests, which are thought of as natural dividing lines between countries. This vision, as it naturalises borders, contributes to increasing their political stability.

2.1.2 Borders as zones: "in between" spaces

The first conception of borders which we presented stems from a State-centric vision which doesn't take into account the multi-level nature of borders as national but also as local and international objects, which are influenced by fluxes at all these different levels.

Contrary to this first vision, interactions which can be observed between communities in borderlands depend both on the relation which States entertain at central level and on the one that borderlanders develop at the local level. These two factors jointly influence the level of control and of interrelations which can be observed locally in the borderlands (OSÓRIO MACHADO, 1998). Aron (1962, p. 278), referring to the Franco-German border, emphasises the importance of relations between neighbours at the local level: "The stability of borders depends on physical and strategic elements only to a very limited degree: it is a result of the relationship of the communities that it separates".

The relation which the inhabitants of these regions have with the border is daily, much more immediate and intimate than that of populations living in central areas of the country. For them, it is an interface which structures daily life (FOUCHER, 2019).

Furthermore, the much closer contact they have with populations from the neighbouring country makes this relation necessarily different from that of inhabitants living in the centres of both countries. As social identity is a result of one's social relations (VAN HOUTUM; LAGENDIJK, 2001), borderlands often constitute "places of multiple fusions, of blood and cultures" (ALBUQUERQUE, 2005, p. 38) in which integration with the neighbouring country is stronger than it is in the centre of the country.

Thus, another conception of the border emerges, focused less on separation and rather on the connection between two units. It is therefore seen as a zone of overlapping (WILLE et al., 2015; WILLE, 2015), an *in between space*. Flusser sees border zones as spaces in which neighbouring regions have a special tie. Based on this connection, border regions are described as "grey zones" (WILLE et al., 2015, p. 22) in which characteristics overlap. Other authors such as Kalscheuer talk about zones of cultural exchange in which conflicting images of the self and of the other are negotiated (WILLE et al., 2015).

The notion of borderland, later adopted by border studies scholars, was coined by the Chicana[1] poet Gloria Anzaldúa in Borderlands/La Frontera: The New Mestiza (1987). She presented the term as follows:

A border is a dividing line, a narrow strip along a deep edge. The borderlands are a vague and undetermined place created by the emotional residue of an unnatural boundary. It is a constant place of transition. The prohibited and forbidden are its inhabitants.

(ANZALDÚA, 1987, p. 3)

The word was then borrowed by border studies scholars who formulated the concept of borderlands, defined by Newman (2011, p. 37) as,

areas in proximity to the border which constitute a transition zone between two distinct categories, rather than a clear cut-off line. It is an area within which people residing in the same territorial or cultural space may feel a sense of belonging to either one of the two sides, to each of the two sides, or even to a form of hybrid space in which they adopt parts of each culture and/or speak both languages.

This concept focuses on the cultural and/or linguistic ties which exist between the two contiguous spaces, even if the border which separates them impedes the creation of a functional region. Culturally, these zones are transition spaces in which it is possible to observe "a continuum from the absolute characteristics of one group to the absolute characteristics of the other" (NEWMAN, 2011, p. 38).

The vision of the border which is prevalent amongst International Relations scholars with a transnational approach is closest to the one exposed in this section. The border retains its importance for the State, but its role is viewed differently: from a line serving exclusively as a barrier separating "us and them", it acquires the role of a bridge. Thus, in border cities, traditional border infrastructure aiming to control fluxes comes to coexist with border-crossing facilities and transborder cooperation (MORACZEWSKA, 2010).

The dynamics of border zones as integrated and potentially cooperating spaces can be the result of two types of processes. On the one hand, cross-border integration can be a bottom-up process based on immediate, human, everyday interaction between borderlanders[2]. On the other hand, it can also be a top-down process led by individuals situated at the centre of the State, through tools ranging from agreements, laws and policies to official events (BENTO, 2015). Most often, cross-border integration is the result of a combination of both processes, though some authors argue that top-down integration is ineffective without the previous existence of a bottom-up dynamic (BENTO, 2015; LERESCHE; SAEZ, 1997). However, the bottom-up dynamic does not need its counterpart in order to exist; the top-down process will legitimise, institutionalise and facilitate it. This is particularly felt by borderlanders in services which are highly dependent on geographic proximity such as health, social services and education and in which the creation of specific legal frameworks and infrastructure helps to overcome the inadequacy of many national policies and services in the context of borderlands (BENTO, 2015).

Within this vision of borders as transitional spaces shaped as zones, various different delimitations can be made between a number of terminologies and corresponding spaces or visions of the space.

A border region, in a national perspective, corresponds to an area in which a concentration of cross-border fluxes can be found. A border zone is a junction of two or more border regions of neighbouring countries (STEIMAN, 2002). It can be defined more precisely as "a geographic space constructed by border networks and fluxes, which can vary based on the result produced by the contact between the countries" (FURTADO, 2011, p. 35). These two concepts are therefore based on interactions.

Researching borderlands: shifting the focus 13

These interactions can be of two types: spontaneous, in the case of informal networks and fluxes, and organised, if the State formalises them, thus producing changes in the way it perceives the border and on the region's territorial order (OSÓRIO MACHADO, 1998). Examples of such State actions which have been put in place on the Brazilian territory are free trade areas, free-trade zones or dry ports.

Some States give a legal formalisation to this vision of the border as a zone, through the creation of what we will refer to as a border strip – an area alongside the borderline to which is attributed a differentiated political treatment in relation to the rest of the national territory, based on the special characteristics which it is considered to have. In South America, six countries operate this legal differentiation in relation to border areas: Brazil, Uruguay, Paraguay, Bolivia, Peru and Ecuador. Despite the fact that the existence of a border strip is usually associated to security issues, there are no international standards in terms of size of the strips and norms associated to them: they are defined individually by each State (FURTADO, 2011).

For example, in Brazil, a border strip[3] seen as a national security zone has been defined[4] as a 150 km-wide zone parallel to the national territorial limits. In Uruguay, the border strip[5] delimits an area of 20 km parallel to the border line, in a socio-economic perspective (FURTADO, 2011).

In France, the border strip isn't defined in such a clear-cut way. Some parts of the border are regulated based on a special status of "border zone", whereas others aren't. Some border strips are defined as corresponding to a certain number of kilometres from the dividing line, whereas others include entire regions if they are situated alongside a border. In the case of the Franco-German border, the strip is defined as including 30 km on the German side, 20 km on the French side, as well as the entire départements* of Upper Rhine, Lower Rhine and Moselle.

2.1.3 Borders as relational spaces: where "us" and "them" are connected and separated

Based on their proximity to the border and to neighbouring populations on the other side of the border (as outlined in Section 2.1.2), local populations do not perceive spatial and social boundaries according to the same categories as government officials (NEWMAN; PAASI, 1998). In general terms, the socio-spatial consciousness of borderlanders and its concrete manifestations in art, monuments, landscapes and educational programmes can be different from the one which is carried nationally (PAASI, 2013).

The conceptualisation of this different relationship to space which borderlanders have is challenging for social scientists as they have tended to operate under the assumption of the naturality of the division of space, as well as the connection of the notions of nation, identity and space. For this reason, any conceptualisation of the territorialisation of these "spaces on the edge" or

---
* departments, in English

"in-between spaces" is a challenge: they cannot be analysed according to fixed categories.

From a vision of borders as lines of separation to a vision of them as zones, we come to see them as spaces which are fundamentally linked to relationality, both empirically and symbolically. This relationality, on a practical level, permeates profoundly life in borderlands, since they constitute "zones of mutual interpenetration and constant manipulation of distinct social, political and cultural structures" (OSÓRIO MACHADO, 1998, p. 42).

Foucault (1998, p. 73) emphasises the interdependence between the notion of limit and the act of crossing it:

> The limit and transgression depend on each other for whatever density of being they possess: a limit could not exist if it were absolutely uncrossable and, reciprocally, transgression would be pointless if it merely crossed a limit composed of illusions and shadows.

In his vision, limits do not exist without the possibility of crossing them, and transgression does not exist outside of the existence of limits, be they physical or symbolic. According to this logic, crossing a limit does not imply its disappearing or even its questioning, but a way of experimenting it: by being crossed, it can be felt.

Doll and Gelberg (WILLE et al., 2015) interrogate how Walter Benjamin's image of the "threshold" to describe the transition zones that border spaces constitute can be used to reflect on how two units which are both connected and separate relate to each other. In this sense, border spaces are understood as places of passage.

This relational vision of borders brings with it an acknowledgement of contradictory movements and practices which take place in border regions. As highlighted by Rosenau (1997, pp. 6–7),

> the Frontier is a terra incognita that sometimes takes the form of a market, sometimes appears as a civil society, sometimes resembles a legislative chamber, periodically is a crowded town square, occasionally is a battlefield, increasingly is traversed by an information highway, and usually looks like a several-ring circus in which all these - and many other - activities are unfolding simultaneously [...] in which background often becomes foreground, time becomes disjointed, nonlinear patterns predominate, organizations bifurcate, societies implode, regions unify, markets overlap, and politics swirl about issues of identity, territoriality, and the interface between long-established patterns and emergent orientations.

In his vision, the frontier is actually "a host of diverse frontiers" in which "different issues widen or narrow the Frontier" (ROSENAU, 1997, pp. 6–7). The border's function is seen as fragmegrative – a concept which seeks to describe the joint influence of integrative and disintegrative processes, in which the border is simultaneously permeable to some factors and impermeable to others.

Based on the relational vision of borders exposed in this section, the various contradictory practices which coexist in border spaces can be summarised as follows (Table 2.2):

Table 2.2 Coexisting diverging and converging practices in border spaces

Diverging practices		Converging practices
Separation	⟷	Crossing
Conflict	⟷	Integration
Rejection	⟷	Hybridity

Credit: Solène Marié

For the reasons highlighted previously, border spaces are host to a range of unique phenomena which are only encountered in these regions. But according to Medick, they also produce specific patterns of behaviour because of the fact that State sovereign authorities treat them in special ways. (WILLE et al., 2015, p. 17).

2.1.4 Borders and border spaces as institutions: where "us", "them" and "we" are formalised and performed

Borders constitute institutions in a variety of ways. As presented metaphorically by Henk Van Houtum (2011, p. 51), "The border makes and is made. Hence, a border is a verb".

Firstly, they constitute territorial institutions as markers of national territorial limits as well as rules regarding life on and around these limits. Their relevance and importance in this sense stems from the fact that the territorial principle is a general organising principle of both social and political life (ANDERSON; O'DOWD, 1999). Furthermore, borders are also institutions in the political, legal and administrative sense. As demonstrated previously, they mark the edge of State sovereignty and administrative authority, as established in legal documents. In this sense, they are "territorial discontinuities with a function of political delineation" (FOUCHER, 2009, p. 22).

Furthermore, they constitute historical institutions. Foucher (2009, p. 27) describes borders as "time inscribed in space", as places marked by past or present conflict and therefore places of memory, "somehow just a fading memory" as formulated by Walker (2016, p. 17). Furthermore, as institutions, they include a number of rules which tend towards self-perpetuation and continuity rather than change (NEWMAN, 2003). Thus, they are historical legacies in political and social terms, but also in legal and administrative terms.

Finally, borders constitute discursive institutions: beyond the differentiation of territory, politics and histories, they perform a discursive institutionalisation of difference. What matters the most in the study of the ontology of borders therefore isn't the border itself but the practices which are attached to it: their objectification and the associated power practices which create their reality and meaning (HOUTUM, 2011). Indeed, territorial strategy, as well as a classification of space, constitutes spatial communication and control which contribute to the reification of power (HOUTUM; NAERSSEN, 2002). As spaces which are controlled and delimited by sovereign authority, borderlands are subjected to local discourses around space as well as to discourses coming from the centres of power which may be more or less perceptible symbolically and physically in space (PAASI, 1996). This materialisation and symbolisation conducted around borders can even be qualified as performative. A border is, "for the State, a theatre in which the legitimacy of its power is scrutinized" (FOUCHER, 2009, p. 25). Thus, this classification of space and power is designed not only for internal representational and discursive purposes but also for external projection.

Borders constitute social institutions which embody norms and values (both explicit and implicit) (NEWMAN; PAASI, 1998). Thus, through their symbolic nature, "boundaries both create identities and are created through identity" (NEWMAN; PAASI, 1998, p. 194). Territorial socialisation[6], which consists in a narrative process through which social life is *storied* by social and political institutions based on their relative social power locally, is particularly sensitive in borderlands. As spaces relating simultaneously to the local, national and international spheres, they are subjected to various discourses originating from these different spheres. Through their narrativity of space, institutions, media and educational institutions contribute to molding physical and symbolic territory, through literary landscapes which "shape mindscapes and the perceptual images of the observer" (NEWMAN; PAASI, 1998, p. 197).

A recent phenomenon is the existence, in Western Europe, of experiences of institutionalised cross-border spaces. Though integrated cross-border spaces are not new since the full and complete closing of borders has only rarely been achieved, they are new as a structured, strategic policy object.

Cross-border regions are defined by Perkmann and Sum as "a territorial unit that comprises contiguous subnational units from two or more nation-states" (PERKMANN; SUM, 2002, p. 3). Though they most often are not regions in the legal and political sense and do not possess a dedicated bureaucracy, they can possess alternative forms of governance, which function in similar ways to networks (PERKMANN; SUM, 2002).

Table 2.3 sums up the various ways in which borders can be seen as constituting institutions:

Table 2.3 Different facets of the institutional nature of borders

Borders as institutions	
Territorial	Markers of national territorial limits based on the territorial principle as a general organising principle of both social and political life
Historical	Historical legacies in political and social terms as well as in legal and administrative terms
Discursive	Discursive institutionalisation of difference for internal and external representational purposes
Social	Narrative processes through which life is *storied* by social and political institutions, based on their relative social power locally (territorial socialisation)
Cross-border	Forms of governance oriented towards the integration of contiguous subnational units from two or more nation states

Credit: Solène Marié

2.1.5 Conclusion

Following this exposition of various aspects and conceptions of borders and border spaces, the various existing visions can be summarised visually the following way (Figure 2.4):

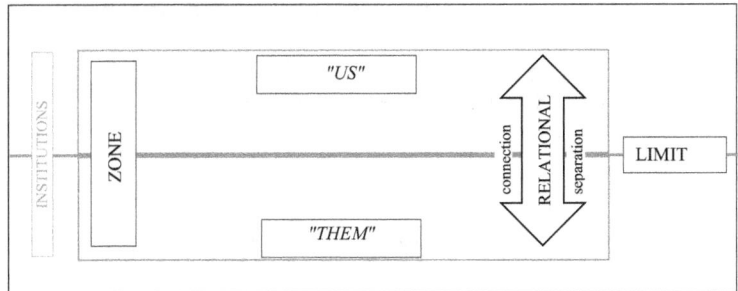

Figure 2.4 Representation of the various dimensions of borders and border spaces

Credit: Solène Marié

Existing literature tends to adopt a vision of borders which relates more to one of the conceptions (borders as lines, as zones, as relational spaces or as institutions) or to look at them one at a time. However, the vision adopted here is that of spaces which combine all these dimensions, which are not mutually exclusive and tend to alternate depending on practices, time and actors involved.

One of the dimensions of borders is their existence as static lines which mark a limit between an inside and an outside, a separation between entities.

18 Researching borderlands: shifting the focus

Another way in which borders can materialise is as zones marked by hybridity, which can develop based on the daily interaction between neighbouring populations. These are marked by cooperation which can stem from local processes and/or of institutionalised dynamics involving agents outside of the border space. This vision of borders as zones can also be the result of a securitarian outlook cast on border spaces by State centres. Thirdly, relationality, be it of a practical or of a symbolic nature, is fundamental to border space dynamics. The notions of limit and of crossing are interdependent as one cannot exist without the other; therefore, life in border spaces is marked by the practice of constantly crossing physical and social limits. It is also marked by the contradictory coexistence of converging and diverging practices, which materialises the switches between alternating visions of the border, as exposed previously. Finally, borders constitute territorial, historical, discursive, social and sometimes cross-border institutions.

Figure 2.5 displays visually the way in which these various conceptions of the border shape the coexistence of notions of *us* and *them* in border spaces. Within this framework, institutions (discursive and/or political) can reinforce one of these three visions.

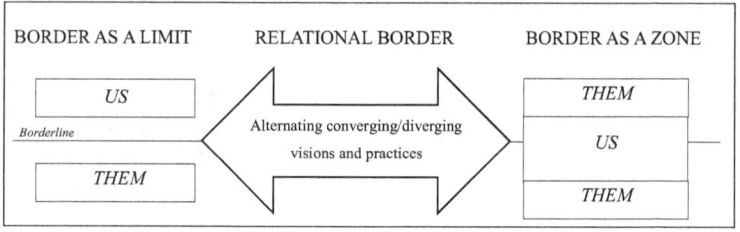

Figure 2.5 Representation of coexisting visions of *us* and *them* in border spaces
Credit: Solène Marié

As highlighted by Walker (2016, p. 1), "boundaries elude any singular logic, topology or conventional account of what it means to understand political phenomena dialectically". Based on this multiplicity of coexisting and sometimes conflicting logics, he adopts a variety of terms (border, boundary limit) which seek to capture these different aspects. Instead, our posture is that of referring only to borders (or borderlands when mentioning the space rather than the line), using the most generic terms as categories. However, within these categories, we distinguish the various and sometimes opposing practices which they encompass and which, together, make up the complexity of this object of study.

Finally, it is important to note that, though our approach to our object is diverse, we are only looking at international borders and their different aspects. This study does not encompass borders between other types of units or metaphorical borders. Furthermore, contrary to existing visions which suggest that borders and States are now disappearing or irrelevant, we do not argue that this is the case. Our aim is to uncover dynamics which sometimes conflict with State action, but which also coexist with it. Though State dynamics and borders are undeniably changing significantly, they have not disappeared.

2.2 Studying cultural issues in borderlands: between anthropology and public policy

As a multifaceted and polysemic notion, culture is very complex to define. So much so that it has been labelled as "something complicated", "a term that no one knows how to explain", "a question impossible to define, identify and describe unambiguously" (Eagleton, 2016; Lane and Ersson, 2005; Weber, 2014 apud. FERREIRA; LIRA, 2019, pp. 1–2), "one of the two or three most complicated words in the English language" (Williams, 1983 apud. WALKER, 1990).

Beyond the fact that the concept of culture is difficult to define, cultural factors are difficult to separate from other factors and thus to isolate as variables (KEATING, 2008). Therefore, culture is also difficult to operationalise empirically and there is a risk of treating it "as a catch-all device that tries to explain everything and succeeds in explaining nothing" (KEATING, 2008, p. 113).

The UNESCO (United Nations Educational, Scientific and Cultural Organization) itself, in the first publication of its series *Studies and Documents on Cultural Policies* produced in 1969 under the title *Cultural Policy: A Preliminary Study*, states that "The participants to the round-table meeting on cultural policies decided unanimously against embarking on an attempt to define culture" (UNESCO, 1969, p. 10). This shows how arduous and complex the task is, as well as possibly of little use.

Within existing definitions, an evolution from the prevalence of a humanist definition of culture focused on human intellect and creativity channelled through the arts to an anthropological notion of culture can be identified from the mid-twentieth century (REEVES, 2004).

The most prominent definition within this second category would be the semiotic one given by anthropologist Clifford Geertz. He defines culture as "webs of significance that [man] himself has spun" (1973, p. 5) which are identifiable as

> an historically transmitted pattern of meanings embodied in symbols, a system of inherited conceptions expressed in symbolic forms by means of which men communicate, perpetuate, and develop their knowledge about and their attitudes toward life.
>
> (GEERTZ, 1973, p. 89)

20 Researching borderlands: shifting the focus

Geertz claims that this concept is neither ambiguous nor multiple and vague as it does not refer to meanings locked in people's heads but can be identified through external symbols that they use.

Looking at culture from a humanist point of view brings us to the examination of cultural policy, which aims to give support to human artistic production. Table 2.4 juxtaposes various definitions of cultural policy commonly used in the literature on the topic, summarising in a few words the interpretation that they make of the actors involved and their scope of action.

French literature on the subject, based on Sociology of Public Action's[7] importance in the country, distinguishes "cultural actions" from "cultural policy". Cultural action, in this context, is made up of contributions by various actors from the government-supported cultural and arts sectors without an explicit strategy. Urfalino (2004, p. 14) conceives of cultural policy as "a

Table 2.4 Definitions and interpretations of cultural policy

Author	Definition	Interpretation
UNESCO (1969)	"the sum total of the conscious and deliberate usages, action or lack of action in a society, aimed at meeting certain cultural needs through the optimum utilization of all the physical and human resources available to that society at a given time" (p. 10)	Deliberate societal action Cultural needs
Schuster (2003)	The totality of a government's activities "with respect to the arts (including the for-profit cultural industries), the humanities, and the heritage" (p. 1)	Governmental action Culture in the humanist sense (arts, humanities, heritage)
Rentschler (2002)	Governmental strategies and activities that promote "the production, dissemination, marketing, and consumption of the arts" (p. 17)	Governmental action throughout the chain of production/consumption Culture in the humanist sense
Miller and Yúdice (2002)	"the institutional supports that channel both creativity and collective ways of lives [...] embodied in systematic, regulatory guides to action that are adopted by organisations to achieve their goals" (p. 1)	Institutional support and regulation Culture in the humanist and anthropological sense
Saez (1993)	"a temporary agreement on a social definition of culture, of its function in society and the individuals who are a part of it, as well as a desire to act upon this object" (p. 45)	Societal action to support culture

Credit: Solène Marié

moment of convergence and consistency between representations of the role which the State can give to arts and culture with regards to society, and the organisation of public action".

The notion of cultural action is therefore closer to wider definitions of cultural policy, such as the ones by the UNESCO (1969) and Saez (1993) included in Table 2.4. As highlighted by Schuster (2003, p. 9), a large proportion of cultural policy results from "actions and decisions taken without expressed policy intention" by a large number of agents who do not compose a conceptual whole nor always fully understand the general impact of their actions, as well as in the form of varied administrative actions. A wider conception of cultural policy is the one favoured here, as further developed in Section 3.2.3.

2.3 Borders and culture: who says what, where and how?

2.3.1 Border scholarship: the development of border studies

Borders are objects which can be studied within various disciplines and therefore in line with a variety of approaches: they span geography, history, economy, anthropology, ethnology, political science, law, psychology, sociology and other social sciences (NEWMAN; PAASI, 1998; BRUNET-JAILLY, 2005). Border scholarship now even sometimes draws connections with philosophy, ethics and cultural, critical, gender, art and media studies (STAUDT, 2017; KOLOSSOV; SCOTT, 2013).

However, this field's roots are mainly in geography and more specifically in geopolitics. In the first half of the twentieth century, these scholars were already debating border issues, setting the premises of the debates at the foundation of border studies. Ellen Churchill Semple claimed that natural frontiers were ideal boundaries, contrary to those established through human action. Albert Brigham alleged that borders provided economic equilibrium, Whittermore Boggs that they lessened intra-State tensions, Nicholas Spykman that borderlands probably played a fundamental role in the understanding of inter-state relations and Roderick Peattie that they strengthened State power (apud. BRUNET-JAILLY, 2010). On the basis of this previous debate conducted mainly by geographers, the field of border studies developed from the 1970s as a fundamentally changing and interdisciplinary one.

Initially grounded in an empirical tradition which emphasised historical-geographical contingency, it shifted towards the creation of models and an aim for generalisation with the development of positivist thinking. With the rise of behaviourism, psychological aspects related to the perception of borders were introduced into border scholarship. Finally, during the 1990s, post-structuralist and ethnographic approaches were incorporated and were the basis for the interdisciplinary evolution of the field (PAASI, 2011). Today, it can be said to have generally taken a postcolonial/postmodern turn (STAUDT, 2017).

2.3.2 Trends and main issues in the field

The study of borders has been marked, for a long time, by a difference of perspectives and of preferred themes depending on scholars' disciplinary positioning, and this disciplinary bias is still present despite the move towards interdisciplinarity. Anthropologists and ethnologists tend to focus on borderlanders' cultural and identitarian issues and to view borders in a mostly metaphorical sense. Economists tend to focus on questions of trade and taxation. Political scientists and internationalists tend to cast a State-centric look on border issues and to take them as a given as lines separating sovereign States in the international system. However, a certain number of International Relations scholars started questioning this posture in the 1990s and were joined by critical geopoliticians (SHAPIRO, ALKER, 1996; Ó TUATHAIL, DALBY, 1998).

The consequence of this heterogeneity is the coexistence of various views and explanations for the same phenomena, which renders theorisation difficult: "there have been few attempts to formulate models that would encompass this diverse scholarship's range of analytical concerns" (BRUNET-JAILLY, 2005, p. 634). Different scholars reach different conclusions as to the determining factors of cross-border integration: culturally embedded explanations by geographers and historians emphasise the role of local communities; political scientists insist on the role of institutions; and rationalist explanations developed by economists identify economic processes as fundamental, linked to the structural role of the border as a divider between two markets. Yet other explanations emphasise the role of language and ethnicity and the role of local actors, of central governments and of religion (BRUNET-JAILLY, 2010). Though the interdisciplinary field of border studies now exists since the 1990s, it still seems that border scholars and scholars from other disciplines working on borders are "travelling forward in different trains" (PAASI, 2013).

Whilst some authors, based on the diversity of border research, claim that no common elements can be found within the set of borders which have been studied (PRESCOTT, 1987), others claim that border theory can indeed be expanded and developed (ALPER; BRUNET-JAILLY, 2008) through the creation of models (e.g., BRUNET-JAILLY, 2004; BRUNET-JAILLY, 2005) or border theories (e.g., NEWMAN, 2003). There is a debate as to how this generalisation could take place given the diversity of cases, such that some political geographers have suggested that theorisation should focus on boundary-producing practices rather than on the borders themselves (Ó TUATHAIL, 1996; Ó TUATHAIL; DALBY, 1998; PAASI 1996; PAASI, 2011; NEWMAN, 2003).

Another salient issue in border studies is that, compared to other concepts in the social sciences, borders have generated relatively little conceptualisation (NEWMAN; PAASI, 1998) and therefore suffer from a certain lack of clarity in their definition or agreement on the latter. As emphasised by Newman (2011, p. 44), "An important step in this respect is the creation of a common language, or glossary of terms, which are recognizable by border scholars, regardless of their specific compartmentalized discipline". Borders tend to be taken either in a very literal and unquestioned sense (mostly within Political Science and International Relations) or in a mostly metaphorically one (especially within Sociology, Psychology and Literature).

Furthermore, border scholarship suffers from a certain lack of historical perspective as "border scholars more often than not seem to be interested in the present situation prevailing in border areas rather than tracing borders as historically contingent processes" (PAASI, 2011). Furthermore, existing models tend not to address the variable of the length of time a border has been in existence (STAUDT, 2017).

Finally, a major issue in border studies is the fact that it is produced mainly in Northern countries. According to a study conducted by Pisani, Reyes and García Jr, of all articles published in the *Journal of Borderlands Studies* between its creation in 1986 and 2008, 13% of all published articles and 44.9% of all multi-authored works derived from multidisciplinary research teams. This percentage is relatively low given that this journal explicitly states its multidisciplinary orientation since its creation.

Beyond the limits linked to discipline-specific explanations and to diverging approaches, border literature is often the result of single-case empirical studies conducted in research centres situated in the Global North. Pisani, Reyes and Garcia's study shows that 72.7% of the articles included in the study were written by researchers based in North America (the USA and Canada) and 18.5% in Europe. This leaves 8.4% of the publications for other parts of the world. Scholarship from Latin America originates exclusively from Mexico with 4.7% and Venezuela with 0.4% (PISANI; REYES; GARCÍA JR, 2009).

As the study of borders relies on case studies and "many topics do not lend themselves to random samples (i.e., informality), the lack of generalizable research is a weakness" (PISANI; REYES; GARCÍA JR, 2009, p. 12). Amongst the publications included in the aforementioned study, approximately half can be categorised as applied research, whilst one quarter is conceptual/theorising and the rest presents a mix of both. This shows the preponderance of an applied approach within the field.

More specifically, "research in border studies has relied mainly on generalisations from cases in the US-Mexico borderlands" (STAUDT, 2017, p. XXV). As it is the border which has traditionally been the most studied and therefore has many university departments specialised in the theme, publications on borders originate mainly from that region. As an illustration of this, the first nine universities which contributed the most to the *Journal of Borderlands Studies* in 2008 were from that region (BRUNET-JAILLY, 2010). Consequently, border models and general border scholarship tend to be greatly influenced by the specific configuration of that border.

The combination of these elements has various consequences. Firstly, these studies lack generalisability. Secondly, scholarship tends to "assume the constant of a strong 'state', with the semblance of democracy and good governance, rather than to evaluate the reality of strong to weak, failed, and/ or absent states" (STAUDT, 2017, p. 43). In the latter and generally in Southern countries, the institutionalisation of border regions may take on a different meaning or be resisted or encouraged for reasons other than those which would prevail in the North. The premise that an interdependent border will develop into an integrated one also assumes the existence of democracies and good governance and therefore does not apply to most borders in the world. For all these reasons linked to the regional concentration of research, there is a lack of views from Southern borders and of cross-regional analysis and thus a need to "become aware of borders in other world regions, comparing their similarities and differences" (STAUDT, 2017, p. 9).

This statement, coming from an English-language scholar and book, points towards an apparent lack of studies coming from academic centres other than North America and Europe and a possible lack of dialogue between scholars. Thinking about this issue from a South American viewpoint, it appears that even compared to other regions in the Global South, the literature on South American borders is scarce. Works in English focusing on rarely studied or Southern borders include few examples from this region (STAUDT, 2017; ALPER; BRUNET-JAILLY, 2008).

Notes

1 Term used to refer to a chosen identity claimed by some Mexican-Americans in the United States. Though it has previously carried a negative connotation, it was reclaimed by the Chicano movement in the 1960s–1970s as a way of affirming ethnic pride, self-determination and solidarity within the Mexican-American community.
2 Name given to inhabitants of borderlands.
3 Faixa de fronteira.
4 Through Law 6634, of 2nd of May 1979, Decree 85.064 of 1980 and article 20, §2 of the federal constitution of 1988.
5 Faja de frontera.
6 Defined as "the process through which individual actors and collectivities are socialized as members of certain territorially bounded spatial entities and through which they more or less actively internalize collective territorial identities and shared traditions" (PAASI, 1996, p. 8).
7 Sociologie de l'Action Publique.

References

ALBUQUERQUE, J. L. C. **Fronteiras em movimento e identidades nacionais: A imigração brasileira no Paraguai**. Doctoral thesis in sociology. Fortaleza: Universidade Federal do Ceará, 2005.

ALPER, D.; BRUNET-JAILLY, E. Special issue: 'Rarely studied borderlands'. **Journal of Borderlands Studies**, v. 23, n. 3, pp. 1–5, 2008.
AMILHAT SZARY, Anne-Laure. Boundaries and borders. In: AGNEW, John et al. [eds]. **The Wiley Blackwell Companion to Political Geography**. Chichester: Wiley Blackwell, 2015, 745p.
ANDERSON, James; O'DOWD, Liam. Borders, Borders Regions and Territoriality: Contraditory Meanings, Change Significance. **Regional Studies**, v. 33, n. 7, pp. 593–604, 1999.
ANZALDÚA, G. **Borderlands/La Frontera. The New Mestiza**. San Francisco: Aunt Lute Books, 1987.
ARON, Raymond. **Paix et guerre entre les nations**. Paris: Calmann-Lévy, 1962.
BENTO, Fábio Régio. Cidades-gêmeas e conurbadas de fronteira: na vanguarda da integração regional. In: PRADO, Henrique Sartori de Almeida; Espósito Neto, Tomaz [org.]. **Fronteiras e relações internacionais**. Curitiba: Ithala, 2015, pp. 101–114.
BLEIKER, R. The aesthetic turn in international political theory. **Millennium: Journal of International Studies**, v. 30, n. 3, pp. 509–533, 2001.
BRUNET-JAILLY, E. Toward a model of border studies: What do we learn from the study of the Canadian - American border ? **Journal of Borderlands Studies**, v. 19, n. 1, pp. 1–12, 2004.
BRUNET-JAILLY, E. Theorizing borders: An interdisciplinary perspective. **Geopolitics**, v. 10, n. 4, pp. 37–41, 2005.
BRUNET-JAILLY, E. The State of Borders and Borderlands Studies 2009: A historical view and a view from the journal of borderlands studies. **The Eurasia Border Review**, v. 1, n. 1, pp. 1–15, 2010.
FERREIRA, T. S. H.; LIRA, V. H. **In Search of a Lost Treasure: Cultural Mapping Studies in the Field of Political Science and International Relations in Brazil**. Revista Brasileira de Política Internacional, 2019.
FOUCAULT, Michel. A preface to transgression. In FAUBION, James D. [ed.]. **Aesthetics, Method and Epistemology**. New York: New Press, 1998, pp. 69–87 [French original 1963].
FOUCHER, Michel. **Fronts et frontières. Un tour du monde géopolitique**. Paris: Fayard, 1991.
FOUCHER, Michel. **Obsessão por fronteiras**. São Paulo: Radical Livros. Tradução de Cecília Lopes, 2009. [Original title: L'Obsession des frontières].
FOUCHER, Michel. Nécessaires frontières. **Constructif**, v. 52, n. Europe, Quelles frontières?, 2019.
FURTADO, R. D. S. **O Estado Fragmentado : uma análise das elites organizacionais do Executivo federal e da abordagem da faixa de fronteira no Brasil**. Universidade de Brasília, Brasília, 2011.
GEERTZ, Clifford. **The Interpretation of Cultures: Selected Essays by Clifford Geertz**. New York: Basic Books, 1973.
HOBSBAWM, Eric J. Etnia e nacionalismo na Europa de hoje. In: BALAKRISHNAN, Gopal [org.]. **Um mapa da questão nacional**. Rio de Janeiro: Contraponto, 2000.
KEATING, Michael. Culture and social science. In: DELLA PORTA, Donatella; KEATING, Michael [ed.]. **Approaches and Methodologies in the Social Sciences**. Cambridge: Cambridge University Press, 2008, pp. 99–117.
KOLOSSOV, V.; SCOTT, J. Selected conceptual issues in border studies. **Belgeo**, v. 2013, n. 1, pp. 0–19, 2013.

KORZYBSKI, Alfred. **Science and Sanity. An Introduction to Non-Aristotelian Systems and General Semantics.** New York: Institute of General Semantics. The International Non-Aristotelian Library, 1st ed., 1933, pp. 747–761.
LERESCHE, J.-P.; SAEZ, G. Identités territoriales et régimes politiques de la frontière. **Pole Sud**, n. 7, pp. 27–47, 1997.
MILLER, Toby; YÚDICE, George. **Cultural Policy.** London: Sage, 2002.
MORACZEWSKA, A. The changing interpretation of border functions in international relations. **Revista Română de Geografie Politică**, v. 7, n. 2, pp. 329–340, 2010.
NEWMAN, David. Boundaries. In: AGNEW, J.; MITCHELL, K.; TOAL, G. [eds]. **A Companion to Political Geography.** Oxford: Blackwell, 2003.
NEWMAN, David. Borders and bordering. **European Journal of Social Theory**, v. 9, n. 2, pp. 171–186, 2006.
NEWMAN, David. Contemporary research agendas in border studies: An overview. In WASTL-WALTER, Doris [ed.]. **The Ashgate Research Companion to Border Studies.** Farnham: Ashgate, 2011.
NEWMAN, D.; PAASI, A. Fences and neighbours in the postmodern world: Boundary narratives in political geography. **Progress in Human Geography**, v. 22, n. 2, pp. 186–207, 1998.
OSÓRIO MACHADO, L. Limites, fronteiras, redes. In: STROHAECKER, T. et al. [eds]. **Fronteiras e espaço global.** Porto Alegre: AGB, 1998, pp. 41–49.
Ó TUATHAIL, G. **Critical Geopolitics.** London: Routledge, 1996.
Ó TUATHAIL, G.; DALBY, S. [eds.]. **Rethinking Geopolitics.** London: Routledge, 1998
PAASI, Anssi. **Territories, Boundaries and Consciousness.** Chichester: John Wiley, 1996.
PAASI, Anssi. A border theory: An unattainable dream or a realistic aim for border scholars? In: WASTL-WALTER, Doris [ed.]. **The Ashgate Research Companion to Border Studies.** Farnham: Ashgate, 2011.
PAASI, A. Borders. In: DODDS, K.; KUUS, M.; SHARP, J. [eds]. **The Ashgate Research Companion to Critical Geopolitics.** Burlington: Ashgate, 2013, 548p.
PERKMANN, M.; SUM, N.-L. [eds]. **Globalization, Regionalization and Cross-Border Regions.** London: Palgrave Macmillan, 2002.
PISANI, M. J.; REYES, J. C.; GARCÍA JR, B. G. Looking back twenty - three years: An analysis of contributors and contributions to the *journal of borderlands studies*, 1986 (volume 1, number 1) to 2008 (volume 23, number 2). **Journal of Borderlands Studies**, v. 24, n. 1, 2009.
PRESCOTT, J.R.V. **Political Frontiers and Boundaries.** London: Allen and Unwin, 1987.
RAFFESTIN, Claude. **Pour une géographie du pouvoir.** Paris: Techniques, 1980, 249p.
REEVES, J. **Culture and International Relations. Narratives, Natives and Tourists.** Abingdon: Routledge, 2004.
RENTSCHLER, Ruth. **The Entrepreneurial Arts Leader: Cultural Policy, Change and Reinvention.** Brisbane: University of Queensland Press, 2002.
ROSENAU, J. **Along the Domestic-Foreign Frontier. Exploring Governance in a Turbulent World.** New York: Cambridge University Press, 1997.
SAEZ, Guy. **L'État, la ville, la Culture.** Thèse en science politique. Grenoble, 1993.

SCHUSTER, J. Mark. **Mapping State Cultural Policy: The State of Washington**. Chicago: The University of Chicago, Cultural Policy Center, 2003.
SHAPIRO, M.J. and ALKER, H.R. [eds]. **Challenging Boundaries**. Minneapolis: University of Minnesota Press, 1996.
STAUDT, Kathleen. **Border Politics in a Global Era**. Lanham: Rowman & Littlefield, 2017.
STEIMAN, R. **Brasil e América do Sul: Questões Institucionais de Fronteira**. Rio de Janeiro: UFRJ, 2002.
UNESCO. **Cultural Policy: A Preliminary Study**. Studies and documents on cultural policies. Paris, 1969
URFALINO, Philippe. **L'invention de la politique culturelle**. Paris: La documentation française, 2004.
VAN HOUTUM, Henk. The mask of the border. In: WASTL-WALTER, D. [ed.]. **The Ashgate Research Companion to Border Studies**. Farnham: Ashgate, 2011.
VAN HOUTUM, H.; LAGENDIJK, A. Contextualising regional identity and imagination on the construction of polycentric urban regions: The cases of the Ruhr area and the Basque country. **Urban Studies**, v. 38, n. 4, pp. 747–767, 2001.
VAN HOUTUM, H.; VAN NAERSSEN, T. Bordering, ordering and othering. **Tijdschrift voor Economische en Sociale Geografie**, v. 93, n. 2, pp. 125–136, 2002.
WALKER, R.B.J. The concept of culture in the theory of international relations. In: CHAY, Jongsuk [ed.]. **Culture and International Relations**. New York: Praeger, 1990.
WALKER, R.B.J. **Out of Line. Essays on the Politics of Boundaries and the Limits of Modern Politics**. New York: Routledge, 2016.
WALTZ, Kenneth N. **Theory of International Politics**. New York: McGraw-Hill, 1979.
WILLE, C. et al. [eds]. **Spaces and Identities in Border Regions. Politics - Media - Subjects**. Bielefeld: Transcript Verlag, 2015.
WILLE, C. **Espaces de frontière. Penser et analyser la frontière en tant qu'espace**: Multilingualism and Intercultural Studies (MIS) Working Paper 4. Université du Luxembourg, 2015.

3 Cultural production in borderlands

Negotiating with the border

3.1 Studying borders within International Relations: (inter)disciplinary constructions

3.1.1 Interdisciplinarity

Currently, the social and symbolic aspects of borders and the "literary narratives" which shape them are mostly studied by scholars working from perspectives and disciplines other than International Relations (IR) or Political Geography. Integrating within mainstream approaches the tools they have developed would, according to Newman and Paasi (NEWMAN; PAASI, 1998, p. 197), considerably enrich border studies:

> Understanding territorial boundaries as a specific type of narrative will considerably broaden the field of concrete boundary studies. This approach suggests that boundaries are not located merely in the empirical contexts of border lines and landscapes, but also in "literary landscapes" which have shaped and continually shape mindscapes and the perceptual images of the observer.

Borders are an intrinsically interdisciplinary object. Therefore, related scholarship also necessarily needs to be: typologies of borders would benefit from more complex transdisciplinary analysis. As pointed out by Walker (2016, p. ix) in *Out of Line*, his collection of essays on the politics of boundaries, these essays "do not have a comfortable disciplinary home; no one interested in the politics of boundaries can afford such luxuries".

Furthermore, an aim which is connected to interdisciplinarity is that of bringing the study of borderlands to an empirical level and to counter the reifying of borders which is very common in the theoretical study of borders within International Relations. Empirically informed perspectives come with an awareness of border processes which counters the tendency of modern scholarly disciplines to take political boundaries "more or less for granted" (WALKER, 2016, p. 15).

3.1.2 Studying the "small things": everyday IR

The understanding of border and borderland dynamics necessarily requires the study of everyday IR. Though the latter are invariably influenced by events, fluxes and actors linked to international and domestic politics, they are not necessarily mediated through them. As Robert Frank (2012, p. XI) phrases it, "International relations are the totality of the relations which human beings and groups establish across borders [...] They aren't limited to war and peace between nations. It is as important to study their 'ordinary' as their 'extraordinary'".

Thus, the study of borderlands requires contemplating the latter as spaces where IR take place, albeit on a different scale, involving different actors and according to different processes than IR studied from the perspective of relations between central governments or global actors. As well as including processes which are not usually studied within mainstream IR and State-centric perspectives, this approach grounded in a borderland perspective brings forth voices which are not frequently heard within mainstream IR: those of borderlanders and of local agents involved in border issues.

Borderlands disturb a number of familiar notions regarding the location of politics, their contents, actors and processes (WALKER, 2016). Their study therefore requires making a number of shifts in perspective.

3.1.3 Breaking the internal/external dichotomy

As Italo Calvino expresses poetically in *Invisible Cities* (1972) in his phrase "Elsewhere is a negative mirror", binarity is present in the way we experience and analyse the world. A dichotomy which is prevalent in IR is that between the internal and the external, the domestic and the international.

R.B.J. Walker, amongst other post-structuralist authors, questions the organisation of world politics around States, be it at the national level (the nation state) or at the international level (a set of territorialised nation states). According to him, the notion of nation state was the modern solution to the problem of particularity/universality. In the postmodern era, new spatio-temporal answers need to be found within the new existing configuration of distances and borders. In this perspective, he defends the idea of going beyond the internal/external dichotomy (WALKER, 1993). Any spatio-temporal concept needs to adapt to the changes of our post-modern era in order to remain relevant and the modern notion of sovereignty is in effect a historically specific form of association of spatiality and temporality (WALKER, 2009).

As highlighted previously, this research seeks to adopt a less State-centric perspective than mainstream IR tends to, seeing borders as mere dividers of sovereign space. However, it envisions neither borders nor States as disappearing, inexistent or irrelevant, such as they have been presented in some recent bodies of literature. These positions reiterate the duality of thinking around borders as "markers of presence or absence" (WALKER, 2016, p. 3).

In effect, current thinking about borders is very much influenced by discriminations which are naturalised because they correspond to predominant and unquestioned notions of the State and sovereignty. They are also taken for granted based on the prevalence of bounded visions of the individual, the state and the international system (WALKER, 2009).

3.1.4 Shifting the focus: from the border "at the edge" to the border "at the centre"

An extensive body of literature, mostly produced in Western Europe, can now be found on the issue of cross-border cooperation and integration, some of it produced by IR or Political Science scholars. However, in most of the research conducted by internationalists, borders are conceived as objects through which IR take place (MORACZEWSKA, 2010). As highlighted by Rosenau, it is time to replace "a boundary that isn't there" with "a new and wide political space" (ROSENAU, 1997, p. 4).

The very notions of integration and cooperation come from the idea of separation: integration and cooperation can only occur between two separate units. Borders, in IR and Political Science, tend to be naturalised and seen as abstractions which are present in space but have very little effect on it (WALKER, 2016). They are seen as the outside layer of the system which the State constitutes: they mark the end of its territory and therefore the limit of its sovereignty as well as its point of contact with the international sphere (MORACZEWSKA, 2010).

Developing research grounded in the borderlands thus implies looking at the border as the centre of another system: that of the borderlands which surround it. Based on this vision, the aim is to analyse territory based on human interactions instead of analysing social phenomena based on fixed categorisations of territory: it is "looking for society's place and not defining society by a given place" (RETAILLÉ, 1996, p. 95).

Figures 3.1 and 3.2 aim to represent the shift in perspective that is operated when situating the system under study within the State or within the borderlands, as well as the shift in the place and role of the border within each system.

Based on our vision of borderlands as exposed in Section 2.1 and on our outlook on them exposed here, we will use the following analytical definition of borderlands: spaces near international borders in which the borderline, border policies or the relational processes inherent in border spaces affect the everyday life of its inhabitants. As these processes vary from one borderland to another as well as within different areas of a specific borderland, the space which it includes on either side of the borderline cannot be defined with a fixed figure. Rather, borderlands take varying forms based on the relationships and networks which can be found across the borderline and their reach throughout space.

Cultural production in borderlands 31

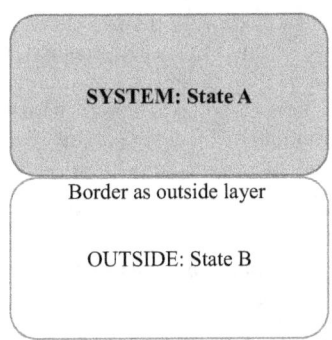

Figure 3.1 Representation of the place of the border within a State-centred system
Credit: Solène Marié

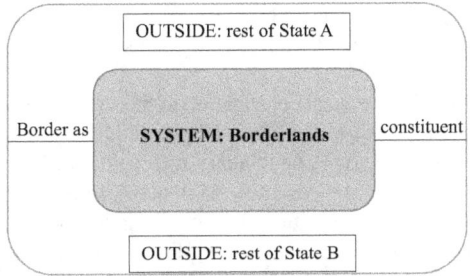

Figure 3.2 Representation of the place of the border within a borderland-centred system
Credit: Solène Marié

As pointed out by Staudt (2017, p. 35), "The size of borderlands is a slippery one, depending on varying local perceptions, government agency rules, and governments". It is important to add that it is also strongly influenced by urbanisation and demography: as the shape of borderlands depends on relationships and networks in existence in space, they will take different shapes depending on whether the areas on either side of the borderline are densely populated urban areas or sparsely populated rural areas, for example.

3.2 Studying culture within IR: what is the object?

In the preface to his book *On Cultural Diversity: International Theory in a World of Difference*, Christian Reus-Smit (2018, p. x) describes a road trip between Europe and Asia made with his parents as a child and he writes, "As we traversed a large swath of Eurasia, the colours, contours, and textures of culture changed, but we didn't step from one hermetically sealed cultural unit to another and we crossed no civilizational border posts. Culture had a topography but no territoriality". Studying culture within the discipline of IR implies defining precisely what it is we will be analysing and how we will operationalise it.

3.2.1 The study of culture in IR: main contributions

Culture is a theme which entered the mainstream of the IR debate quite late, being seen initially as a secondary factor, a by-product of political or economic activity. In the 1950s, Renouvin (1953), moving away from Diplomatic History which he saw as too narrow in its perspective on international history, came to integrate additional sources as well as a new type of thinking around moral and material forces, denominated *deep forces*. By doing this, he created a new methodology for the reading of interactions between people and nations of the world, creating a line of study which analysed these interactions from a historical perspective.

Subsequently, a fundamental contribution to the study of international cultural issues was conducted in the field of Cultural History, which developed in the 1970s through the works of scholars such as Pierre Milza, Michel Espagne and Michael Werner. These historians played a major role in including cultural productions within the study of IR, going beyond the study of representations and including the practical dimension. With the crossing of the disciplines of IR and Cultural History, scholars started looking not only at States' foreign cultural policies but also at all international cultural exchanges, which they called "cultural transfers".

In the 1980s, the theme was also put forward by Marcel Merle. He suggested the creation of a new IR paradigm focused on culture, which he considered a central factor to explain international actors' behaviour. At the time, the cultural factor often appeared in IR theories but generally as a secondary factor.

Within the mainstream of IR, it is in the 1990s that culture entered the debates. In the United States, where the field of IR is closely connected to Political Science, the main themes have tended to revolve around the Cold War and the fall of communism. However, with the *Cultural Turn*, American scholars began to question themselves on the cultural aspects of IR.

In this context, Akira Iriye developed the concept of cultural internationalism, which is based on three elements: incentives to mutual understanding, cooperation and education (REEVES, 2004). Also in this context, Joseph Nye developed the concept of *soft power* (NYE, 1990) which contributed to bringing the theme of culture closer to the mainstream of IR theory. The introduction of this notion aimed to theorise the fact that *hard power* – military, economic and industrial power – was no longer sufficient in order to ensure a State's influence in the international system. The projection of Soft Power – the power of attraction of a culture or of a political and social model – came to be seen as an element through which States could ensure their influence. In this context, Nye defined *soft power* as the ability for an actor to obtain something based on attraction (carrots) instead of coercion (sticks) via the attractiveness of its ideas, values and culture (NYE, 2004, p. 9).

The inclusion of culture within foreign policy mainly revolves around visions of it in terms of *soft power* or in terms of cultural diplomacy, the latter being more exclusively focused on cultural activities.

In general terms, cultural diplomacy can be defined as "an international actor's attempt to manage the international environment by facilitating cultural transmission across an international boundary" (CULL, 2009, p. 53).

More precisely, cultural diplomacy is multidimensional: it relates both to the economic and to the sociopolitical realms based on the double nature of cultural activities, goods and services. As recognised in the UNESCO's 2005 Convention on the Protection and Promotion of the Diversity of Cultural Expressions, these are both economic based on their commercial value and cultural by the identitarian aspects which they bear. Thus, they are powerful diplomatic tools in a globalised world (STOICA; HORGA, 2016) which can relate either to the pursuit of specific outcomes or to inducing changes in issues or in the identity of actors (SINGH, 2010).

Some authors make a distinction between international cultural relations and cultural diplomacy, seeing the former as including all cultural activities which take place beyond national borders whilst the latter is restricted to international cultural activities with some form of involvement from public institutions (BÉLANGER, 1994). Others go further by distinguishing, within cultural diplomacy, actions which are led directly by public institutions, thus according to foreign policy aims, and those which are led by paragovernmental or private organisations and therefore correspond to the aims of these organisations even though they can be inserted within the general foreign policy framework (MITCHELL, 1986). Making a distinction between types of cultural diplomacy based on the type of actor involved corresponds to the distinction which is made between traditional diplomacy and public diplomacy. Whilst the first type corresponds in general terms to the use of cultural aspects of a country's *soft power* by its diplomatic institutions the second one targets the civil society of a foreign country and is conducted by actors who have easier access to it (MELISSEN, 2005; RIORDAN, 2005).

Robert Frank (2012) adopts a wider definition on the basis of his understanding that there are multiple interactions between the public and private sectors in that field. The cultural diplomacy developed by public agents depends on the intellectual and artistic production of the civil society in terms of intellectual debate, tangible and intangible cultural heritage, and cultural production, whilst private agents involved in international cultural activities often rely on help from the state to develop their projects. In this sense, cultural diplomacy is "the set of means and actors which contribute to the States' cultural foreign policies as well as the cultural actions led by non-State actors" (FRANK, 2012, p. 374). He includes in his definition of cultural diplomacy all actions which aim to create intellectual and cultural complicity networks with elites outside of the country and to create a positive image of the country in order to influence public opinion. Thus, his definition comes under what some scholars would define as international cultural relations since it covers the circulation beyond borders of the practices, symbolic productions or even collective mental representations of a community.

3.2.2 The study of culture within IR: limits

Because of the fact that IR's primary focuses are elsewhere, conventional wisdom has it that culture does not enter IR debates. Actually, "IR scholars talk about culture all the time" (REUS-SMIT, 2019, p. 1), it is "the defining characteristic of the discipline's subject matter" (BEATE, 2003, p. 28). Though this aspect will not be detailed here, culture can be identified in most mainstream schools of IR scholarship, from realism to liberalism and constructivism.

Thus, though it is secondary, the topic of culture is not as absent from IR theory as it can appear to be. It is indeed present in the literature, though it displays "neither careful empirical analysis nor complex theoretical discussion" (WALKER, 1990, p. 7). The problem of the cultural discussion in the field has various dimensions.

Firstly, its multifaceted nature makes it a convenient label to explain phenomena once the primary variables, those most explored within IR, have been used up (WALKER, 1990).

Secondly, in this area, "IR looks like a conservation zoo for concepts long dead in their natural habitats" (REUS-SMIT, 2019, p1). Indeed, IR theorists work with an anachronistic concept of culture which does not take into account evolutions from the last three decades within the specialist fields of cultural studies, sociology and anthropology. These have long abandoned a view of cultures as coherent and bounded entities which provide systems of meaning and practices, such as that which can be found in IR literature across various mainstream schools of thought, be it realism or those which give a larger place to culture such as the English school or constructivism (REUS-SMIT, 2018).

Part of IR scholarship translates its reflection on culture as a reflection on values. Within a discipline which gives a central place to the issue of sovereignty and thus sees the State as the main producer of values, this entails that cultural diversity is tolerated when it corresponds to the limits of the State, and that the latter is the main mediator between different value groups (WALKER, 1990). In contrast with this all-encompassing vision, strands of constructivist literature reflect on cultures in a partitioned way, dividing them into specific norms in order to study causal effects and thus losing the complexity which comes from a holistic vision (REUS-SMIT, 2019). Neither of these two ways of envisaging and studying culture manage to incorporate a vision of culture as multi-layered, changing and relational identifications.

Thirdly, it is based on an unreflected epistemology (BEATE, 2003) and an unresolved duality between universalism and relativism or pluralism. The first pole, embodied by cosmopolitans, emphasises the existence of values which transcend cultural particularities, thus downplaying the importance of cultural issues based on the supposed existence of a global moral community. The other pole, communitarians, argue that moral values and commitments are that which bounds together real communities, and thus, culture becomes the main issue which generates conflict between communities (WALKER, 1990; REUS-SMIT, 2018).

According to Walker, overcoming the challenges linked to these assumptions and duality lies in discarding conventional categories used in IR in order to distinguish between an inside and an outside. Additionally,

> To understand the concept of culture as the product of specific historical transformations is thus to understand that to attempt to come to terms with culture now is to engage with questions of political practice.
> (WALKER, 1990, p. 12)

3.2.3 Operationalising the study of culture

Based on this description of the development of cultural discussions within the field of IR and of a number of limits present in IR scholarship regarding the study of cultural issues, our aim is twofold.

Firstly, it is to generate an operationalised outlook on the notion of culture, focusing on observable facts, actors and actions. Consequently, it does not draw on an anthropological conception of culture. Rather, it aims to focus on cultural production which provides both observable facts and external symbols, representing "meaning in action" (WAGENAAR, 2011) which enables analysis.

Secondly, the aim is to be inclusive in the categories of cultural production included in the study, in order to allow for meaningful analysis of the two cases under study. Thus, it is based on a conception of cultural policy which is in line with the UNESCO's definition:

> the sum total of the conscious and deliberate usages, action or lack of action in a society, aimed at meeting certain cultural needs through the optimum utilization of all the physical and human resources available to that society at a given time.
> (UNESCO, 1969, p. 10)

Also, we include "actions and decisions taken without expressed policy intention" (SCHUSTER, 2003, p. 9) as these constitute a significant proportion of actions in the cultural field. This also makes space for the analysis of the two selected cases using the same categories.

We will refer to these actions as cultural actions, though our understanding of this category does not build on French thinking in terms of cultural action (*action culturelle*) which is specific to a landscape of cultural production which is heavily supported and regulated by public institutions.

Based on this definition, Table 3.1 gives a representation of the way the approach to culture is operationalised in this study:

Table 3.1 Analytical model and observables

Dimensions of analysis	Aspects of cultural action	Observables
People	Human resources	Cultural networks
Practices	Deliberate societal actions	Cultural actions (policies and projects)
Places	Society	Topography of culture
	Physical resources	

Credit: Solène Marié

3.3 Multi-sited ethnography as a tool for the study of everyday IR

As pointed out previously, borders are an inherently interdisciplinary object of study. However, border scholarship, though it joins scholars from different backgrounds, remains more multidisciplinary than interdisciplinary. It is an object of study which has been theorised within various different disciplines that have tended not to communicate with each other, as shown in part by the study of the different concepts used within the field (see Chapter 2). This makes the study of borders less compatible with a variable-based approach, which relies on the existence of a series of ontological givens in order to draw inferences. Rather, it corresponds better to process-driven research which can be conducted based on looser categorisations. The existence of process patterns, defined as "recurrent sequences of interaction observed across any number of domains" (FRIEDRICHS, 2016, p. 78), constitutes the universe of cases from which the researcher can draw an explanation of the observed regularity.

In the present research, the observed pattern which triggered my interest was the following: the existence, in some borderlands, of cultural identities and of networks of cultural action which span both sides of a political dividing line. Based on this initial observation, a universe of cases presenting this feature was identified, and two cases were chosen, namely the borderlands between Brazil and Uruguay and those between France and Germany.

Beyond the existence of this common feature and despite differences between the two cases in terms of relation to conflict and historical process of border constitution, both are characterised by a historical role as buffer space between two regional powers (AMILHAT SZARY, 2010; SIMI, 2018). Following a history of successive integration of these zones within the two neighbouring states and of intense population movements both also currently demonstrate a high level of porosity between the spaces on both sides of the border (CARNEIRO FILHO; LEMOS, 2014) and manifestations of hybrid cultural expressions. Both can thus be seen as constituting borderlands, as defined by Newman (WASTL-WALTER, 2011, p. 37):

> areas in proximity to the border which constitute a transition zone between two distinct categories, rather than a clear cut-off line. It is an area within which people residing in the same territorial or cultural space may feel a sense of belonging to either one of the two sides, to each of the two sides, or even to a form of hybrid space in which they adopt parts of each culture and/or speak both languages.

Building on this general outlook on the cases which pointed towards the use of ethnographic methods, a multi-sited ethnographic approach was set up with the aim of "Connect[ing] the several sites that the research explores along unexpected and even dissonant fractures of social location" (MARCUS, 1995, p. 100).

Based on an approach centred on the actors in order to identify practices and relationships (DUBOIS, 2012), our fieldwork was designed through movement and the following of human and institutional relationships, as well as connections and associations (MARCUS, 1995).

References

AMILHAT SZARY, A. Frontières et intégration régionale en Amérique Latine: sur la piste du chaînon manquant. In: FLAESCH-MOUGIN, C.; LEBULLENGER, J. [eds]. **Regards croisés sur les intégrations régionales Europe/Amériques**. Editions Bruylant, collection Rencontres Européennes, pp. 307–341, 2010.

BEATE, Jahn. The power of culture in international relations. In: GIENOW-HECHT, Jessica C.E.; SCHUMACHER, Frank [ed.]. **Culture and International History**. New York: Berghahn Books, 2003.

BÉLANGER, L. La diplomatie culturelle des provinces canadiennes. **Études Internationales**, v. 25, n. 3, p. 421, 1994.

CALVINO, Italo. **Invisible Cities**. Orlando: Harcourt Brace Jovanovich, 1972.

CARNEIRO FILHO, C.P.; LEMOS, B. de O. Brasil e Mercosul: Iniciativas de cooperação fronteiriça. **ACTA Geográfica**, pp. 203–219, 2014.

CULL, N.J. **Public Diplomacy: Lessons from the Past**. Los Angeles: Figueroa Press, 2009.

DUBOIS, V. Ethnographier l'action publique. Les transformations de l'Etat social au prisme de l'enquête de terrain. **Gouvernement et action publique,** v. 1, n. 1, pp. 83–101, 2012.

FRANK, Robert [org.]. **Pour l'histoire des Relations Internationales.** Paris: Presses Universitaires de France, 2012.

FRIEDRICHS, J. Causal mechanisms and process patterns in international relations: Thinking within and without the box. **St. Antony's International Review,** v. 12, n. 1, pp. 76–89, 2016.

MARCUS, G.E. Ethnography in/of the world system: The emergence of multi-sited ethnography. **Annual Review of Anthropology,** v. 24, pp. 95–117, 1995.

MELISSEN, Jan [ed.] **The New Public Diplomacy: Soft Power in International Relations.** London: Palgrave Macmillan, 2005.

MITCHELL, J.M. **International Cultural Relations.** London: Allen and Unwin. Coll.: «Key Concepts in International Relations», no. 3, 1986.

MORACZEWSKA, A. The changing interpretation of border functions in international relations. **Revista Română de Geografie Politică,** v. 7, n. 2, pp. 329–340, 2010.

NEWMAN, D.; PAASI, A. Fences and neighbours in the postmodern world: Boundary narratives in political geography. **Progress in Human Geography,** v. 22, n. 2, pp. 186–207, 1998.

NYE, Joseph S. Jr. Soft power. **Foreign Affairs,** n. 80, pp. 153–171, 1990.

NYE, Joseph S. Jr. **Soft Power: The Means to Success in World Politics.** New York: Public Affairs, 2004.

REEVES, J. **Culture and International Relations. Narratives, Natives and Tourists.** Abingdon: Routledge, 2004.

RENOUVIN, Pierre [org.], **Histoire des Relations Internationales.** 1 vol., Paris: Hachette, 1994 (originally published in 1953).

RETAILLÉ, Denis. La vérité des cartes. **Le débat,** v. 5, n. 92, 1996, pp. 87–98.

REUS-SMIT, C. **On Cultural Diversity: International Theory in a World of Difference.** Cambridge: Cambridge University Press, 2018.

REUS-SMIT, C. International relations theory doesn't understand culture. **Foreign Policy,** 23rd March 2019 pp. 1–7, 2019.

RIORDAN, Shaun. La nueva diplomacia. **Foreign Policy Edición Española,** n. 7, Feb/Mar 2005.

ROSENAU, J. **Along the Domestic-Foreign Frontier. Exploring Governance in a Turbulent World.** New York: Cambridge University Press, 1997.

SCHUSTER, J. Mark. **Mapping State Cultural Policy: The State of Washington.** Chicago: The University of Chicago, Cultural Policy Center, 2003.

SIMI, G. **Between the Line: The Semiotics of Everyday Life in the Brazil-Uruguay Borderlands.** Doctoral thesis in cultural studies. Nottingham: University of Nottingham, 2018.

SINGH, J.P. **International Cultural Policies and Power.** 1st ed. London: Palgrave Macmillan, 2010.

STAUDT, Kathleen. **Border Politics in a Global Era.** Lanham: Rowman & Littlefield, 2017.

STOICA, Alina; HORGA, Ioan. Culture and paradiplomatic identity: Instruments in sustaining EU policies. In STOICA, Alina; HORGA, Ioan; RIBEIRO, Maria Manuela Tavares [eds]. **Culture and Paradiplomatic Identity: Instruments in Sustaining EU Policies.** Newcastle Upon Tyne: Cambridge Scholars Publishing, 2016.

SUPPO, Hugo Rogelio. O papel da dimensão cultural nos principais paradigmas das Relações Internacionais. In SUPPO Hugo Rogelio, LEITE LESSA Monica [eds]. **A quarta dimensão das relações internacionais: a dimensão cultural.** Rio de Janeiro: Contra Capa, pp. 13–43, 2012.
UNESCO. **Cultural Policy: A Preliminary Study.** Studies and Documents on Cultural Policies. Paris, 1969
WAGENAAR, Hendrik. **Meaning in Action.** Interpretation and Dialogue in Policy Analysis. New York: Routledge, 2011.
WALKER, R.B.J. The concept of culture in the theory of international relations. In: CHAY, Jongsuk [ed.]. **Culture and International Relations.** New York: Praeger, pp. 3–17 1990.
WALKER, R.B.J. **Inside/Outside: International Relations as Political Theory.** Cambridge: Cambridge University Press, 1993.
WALKER, R.B.J. **After the Globe, Before the World.** New York: Routledge, 2009.
WALKER, R.B.J. **Out of Line. Essays on the Politics of Boundaries and the Limits of Modern Politics.** New York: Routledge, 2016.
WASTL-WALTER, Doris. **The Ashgate Research Companion to Border Studies.** Farnham: Ashgate, 2011.

4 Cultural governance in the Brazil-Uruguay borderlands
Policy and activism

4.1 Geographical contextualisation

The border which Brazil shares with Uruguay reaches a total of 1.068 km. It starts at the triple border between Argentina, Brazil and Uruguay, and ends on the Atlantic coast. For Brazil, this border is, in extension, the seventh of the total of ten borders which it shares with neighbours. In terms of relative length, it represents 6.39% of Brazil's 15,700 km of land borders (BRASIL, 2005). For Uruguay, the extension of this border is much more considerable: it represents 68% of the country's 1564 km of land borders.

The maps in Figures 4.1–4.3 indicate the localisation of these borderlands and situate them within the subcontinent and within the La Plata region. The aim of these maps is not to delineate precisely the limits of the borderlands as, in line with our analytical definition of borderlands presented previously,[1] this is not possible. These maps are included for contextualisation and visualisation.

Figure 4.1 Location of the Brazil-Uruguay borderlands within the sub-continent
Credit: Google

DOI: 10.4324/9781003413400-4

Cultural governance in the Brazil-Uruguay borderlands 41

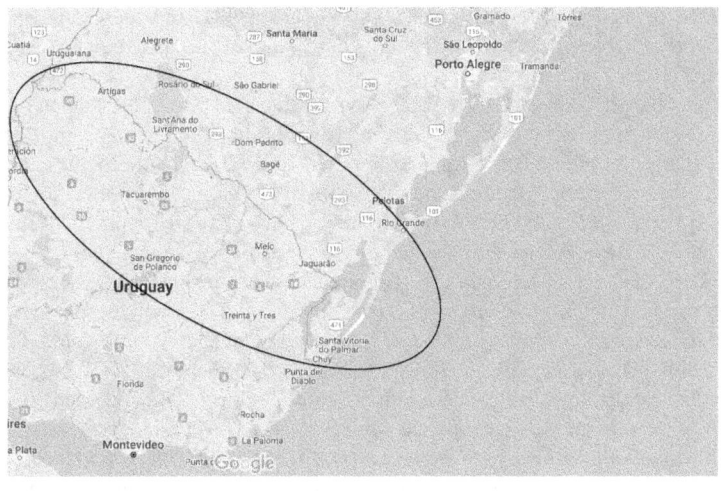

Figure 4.2 Location of the Brazil-Uruguay borderlands within the La Plata region
Credit: Google

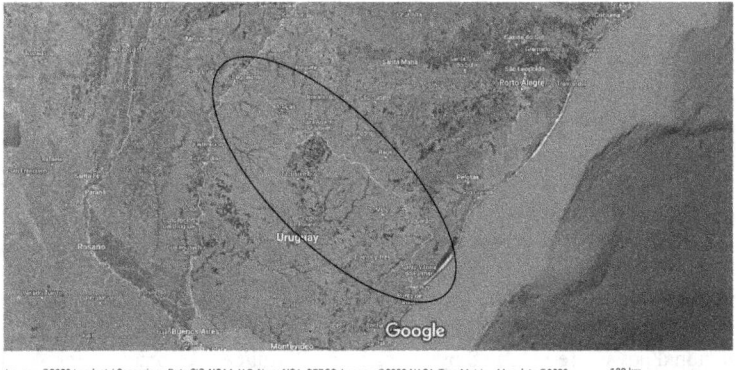

Figure 4.3 Satellite view of the Brazil-Uruguay borderlands within the La Plata region
Credit: Google

In terms of administrative units, this border region includes the *estado* of Rio Grande do Sul (on the Brazilian side) and the *departamentos* of Cerro Largo, Rivera and Artigas (on the Uruguayan side).

As a consequence of historical characteristics of the region, it is intrinsically defined by border characteristics. Whilst Uruguay can be said to constitute a "border State", the southernmost state of Brazil, Rio Grande do Sul, can be defined as a "border state" (OLIVEN, 1999). Given the significant difference between the territorial extensions of Brazil and of Uruguay, these characteristics naturally affect different proportions of the national territory.

The border between Brazil and Uruguay is situated within the Pampa biome, an area of fertile lowlands which corresponds to 75,000 km² spread out over parts of southern Brazil (namely the south of the Rio Grande do Sul state) and of northeastern Argentina and the whole of Uruguay. Within this biome, all the extension of the border region between Brazil and Uruguay is of the Uruguayan Savana type and thus belongs to the same vegetational unit.

For a number of reasons, the geographical characteristics of this region were fundamental in leading to the constitution of a regional social space. Firstly, based on a similar climate as well as favourable conditions for cattle breeding in the spaces situated on both sides of the current location of the border, the borderlands developed relatively similar ways of life and economic activity. Furthermore, geographical conditions were favourable to the establishment of populations. Finally, the absence of impassable barriers in the terrain as well as the presence of rivers and lakes favoured communication and transit of these populations within the area (CLEMENTE, 2010).

4.2 Historical contextualisation

Political borders are the result of historical processes, and thus, their study needs to include the acknowledgement of the profoundly historically contingent nature of border and borderland phenomena and processes (GRIMSON, 2000). Furthermore, borderlands are inherently influenced by fluxes and processes from multiple levels: local, regional, national and international. Thus, contextualising borderlands also implies connecting the history of the region with national and international histories.

The current shape of the border dates back to 1828 when Uruguay obtained independence based on an agreement between Brazil and Argentina with mediation by George Canning, then British Foreign Secretary. This was the end of a history of shifts in the territorial and political affiliation of a region which has historically played the role of a buffer zone between the regional powers represented by Spanish and Portuguese colonial powers, and subsequently by the independent states of Brazil and Argentina. The historical events and patterns which affected this buffer zone will be presented hereafter, not with the intention of providing a full historical analysis of the region but in general terms in order to provide historical context and depth.

Though recounting the history of the region implies giving an account of political and diplomatic processes and events which affected it, this does not imply that the history of the region is limited to the latter. But this specific history does capture the existence and evolution of projects to occupy land and mobilise its population in support for this, projects which therefore affect the history of the borderlands and borderlanders. However, essentialising claims cannot be made based on national status. Furthermore, the categorical nature of such claims is even weaker regarding inhabitants of a zone in which, because of regular changes in the boundary line and therefore in national status, allegiance can be seen as very volatile:

> Not only did jurisdictions change, imposing a scenario where illegality depended less on individuals' decision to break the law and more on the circumstantial reach and location thereof, but people were likewise left with a weak idea of who was in power, which ultimately paved the way to an ongoing condition in which the local has, throughout the centuries, held primacy over the national.
>
> (SIMI, 2018, p. 55)

It is also worth highlighting the fact that, in the South American continent, the relation of antecedence between borders and nations is different to that which prevailed in Europe, in which the idea of nation preceded the delimitation of its territory and borders. In colonised South America, the tracing of borders preceded the construction of a political and social project within the delimited space. The construction of nations was based on appropriation processes in spaces which had been delimited as constituting states (AMILHAT SZARY, 2010).

Furthermore, the tracing of borders in colonised South America did not come with clarity regarding their exact location, as was the case with the delimitation of the border between the Spanish and Portuguese empires in the San Ildefonso Treaty of 1777: maps produced by the two empires at the time displayed different territories and limits.

The *uti possidetis de facto* principle[2] has a significant relevance in the history of South American borders. It can be translated into English as "as you possess, so you may possess", and it considers the current occupier of the land its legitimate owner in the event of a dispute. It can be opposed to *uti possidetis juris*: a principle according to which ownership titles designate the legitimate owner of the land. Though *uti possidetis de facto* had occasionally been used before in colonial times, it came to be adopted as a norm in Brazilian diplomacy in 1849 and was the baseline for Brazilian border politics until the actions of the Baron of Rio Branco[3] (GOES FILHO, 2000, 2013).

Following the May Revolution which led to its independence in 1810, Argentina aimed, through the creation of the United Provinces of the Rio de la Plata,[4] to unite all the territories which had previously made up the Viceroyalty of the Río de la Plata dependencies. In most of the territory which makes up present-day Uruguay, the Spanish were still strong, but there existed a movement of insurgency centred around José Artigas, which the United Provinces gave support to (GOES FILHO, 2000, 2013).

In 1811, Luso-Brazilian troops descended upon Uruguay. They were motivated by their preoccupations regarding the movement and its link to the United Provinces, as well as regarding Artigas's intention to recover the missions[5] which were situated in the strategic territory and were linked to an aim for systematic territorial occupation.

In 1816, with the Spanish having already left Uruguay, the Portuguese General Carlos Frederico Lecor, descended further and took Montevideo on the 20th of January, 1817. In the countryside, confrontation between supporters of Artigas and Luso-Brazilian troops lasted until 1820, when the former were defeated during the battle of Tacuarembó. Based on this defeat, the Banda Oriental[6] was integrated to the Portuguese Empire in 1821 under the name of Cisplatine Province[7] (GOES FILHO, 2000, 2013). In 1822, the Cisplatine Province was integrated to the Brazilian independence process, along with the other provinces.

In 1825, following the takeover of territory by troops led by Juan Antonio Lavaleja, previously Artigas's collaborator, as well as the vote to incorporate Montevideo to the United Provinces, the Brazilian Empire declared war. This war lasted until 1827 when both countries, which were economically weakened and dealing with domestic issues, decided to put an end to it. On the 27th of August 1828, Brazil and Argentina signed a peace treaty which both put an end to the conflict and recognised the independent state of the Oriental Republic of Uruguay.[8]

In 1851, the Treaty of Limits[9] was signed between Uruguay and Brazil, fixing the limits between the two countries based on elements of the establishment of the Cisplatine Province in 1821 and on the *uti possidetis* principle. Thereafter, the Mirim Lagoon came to be of exclusive Brazilian use rather than shared between the two countries.

Through a treaty presented in 1909 by the Baron of Rio Branco, these limits were modified to allow for Uruguayan access to the Mirim Lagoon and to the Jaguarão/Yaguarón River through a shift of the border to the middle of those water courses (Figure 4.4). This was the last significant change in the history of the border between Brazil and Uruguay. In honour of this voluntary territorial concession from Brazil, the Uruguayan government renamed the town of Artigas, which is now called Río Branco in honour of the Baron of Rio Branco.

Figure 4.4 Street sign in Jaguarão, Brazil, twin city situated across the Jaguarão River from Río Branco, Uruguay

Credit: Solène Marié

Cultural governance in the Brazil-Uruguay borderlands 45

Figure 4.5 brings an overview of the main events and treaties which had an effect on the region and of the main shifts in political and territorial affiliation which stemmed from them.

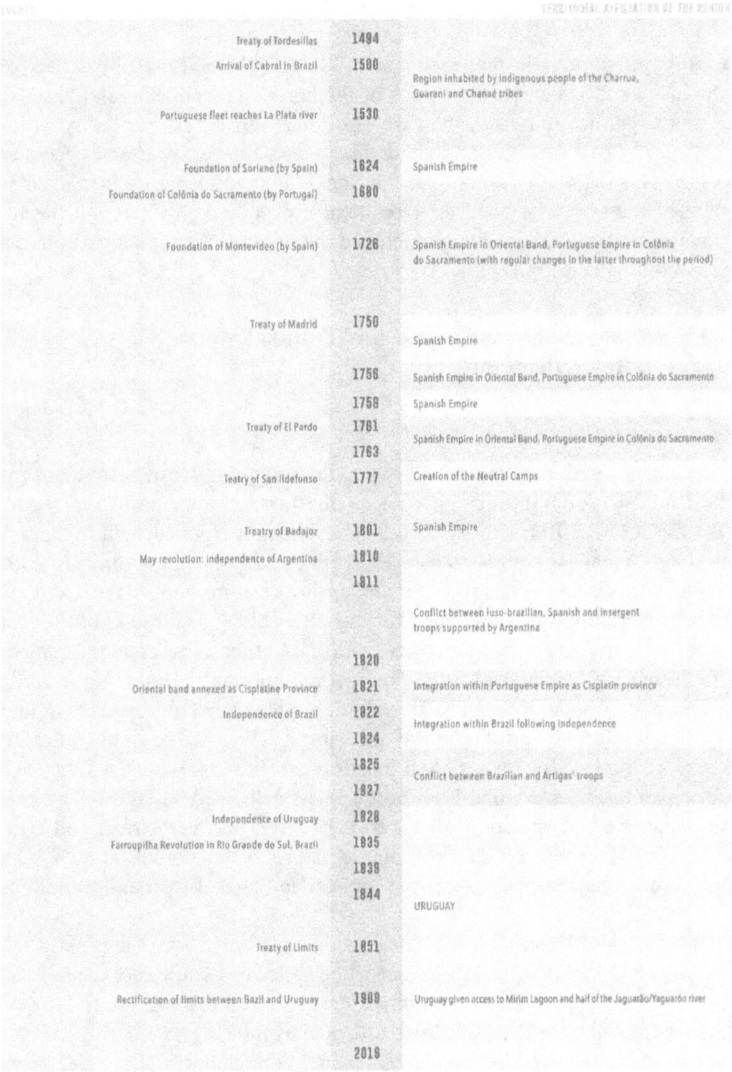

EVENTS		TERRITORIAL AFFILIATION OF THE REGION
Treaty of Tordesillas	1494	
Arrival of Cabral in Brazil	1500	
		Region inhabited by indigenous people of the Charrúa, Guaraní and Chanaé tribes
Portuguese fleet reaches La Plata river	1530	
Foundation of Soriano (by Spain)	1624	Spanish Empire
Foundation of Colônia do Sacramento (by Portugal)	1680	
Foundation of Montevideo (by Spain)	1726	Spanish Empire in Oriental Band, Portuguese Empire in Colônia do Sacramento (with regular changes in the latter throughout the period)
Treaty of Madrid	1750	
		Spanish Empire
	1756	Spanish Empire in Oriental Band, Portuguese Empire in Colônia do Sacramento
	1758	Spanish Empire
Treaty of El Pardo	1761	
	1763	Spanish Empire in Oriental Band, Portuguese Empire in Colônia do Sacramento
Teatry of San Ildefonso	1777	Creation of the Neutral Camps
Treaty of Badajoz	1801	Spanish Empire
May revolution: independence of Argentina	1810	
	1811	
		Conflict between luso-brazilian, Spanish and insurgent troops supported by Argentina
	1820	
Oriental band annexed as Cisplatine Province	1821	Integration within Portuguese Empire as Cisplatin province
Independence of Brazil	1822	
	1824	Integration within Brazil following independence
	1825	
	1827	Conflict between Brazilian and Artigas' troops
Independence of Uruguay	1828	
Farroupilha Revolution in Rio Grande do Sul, Brazil	1835	
	1839	
	1844	URUGUAY
Treaty of Limits	1851	
Rectification of limits between Brazil and Uruguay	1909	Uruguay given access to Mirim Lagoon and half of the Jaguarão/Yaguarón river
	2016	

Figure 4.5 Timeline of the political and territorial affiliation of the region
Credit: Solène Marié and Delphine Perrot

The delimitation of a borderline whose stability was thereafter maintained for more than a century clarified the political dominion over a long-disputed territory. However, this is not to say that its interstitial nature disappeared. As highlighted by Palermo (2019, p. 23), until the beginning of the 19th century, "the territories of the North Band[10] practically represented a territorial, economic and social extension of Rio Grande do Sul".

Clemente (2010) identifies a number of reasons which led to the regionalisation of politics in that area. Firstly, it was characterised by a lack of presence of the State on both sides of the border as well as a total absence of municipal institutions in the case of oriental territories. Furthermore, local political and rebel leaders created networks for civil war and access to power. This regionalisation of politics had a direct influence on the development of the borderlands in their political aspects, notably through the regionalisation of conflicts which included the involvement of actors from the neighbouring country.

4.3 Demographic, economic and cultural contextualisation

4.3.1 Urbanisation of the borderlands

The close relations between the populations living on both sides of the Brazil-Uruguay border go back to the first settlements in the region (FRIZZO; RIBEIRO; DE ÁVILA, 2015). The first cities located in that region were created by both states in the 19th century along the limits of their territory precisely to consolidate it and ensure customs controls (FRANÇA, 2016). Therefore, the location of various cities along or close to the border is not random, and the coexistence with the border is an essential part of life in these borderlands. Furthermore, it is important to note that in these borderlands, the border held chronological precedence over urbanisation: it is the borderline and the aim of securing it which led to the creation of towns on both sides, rather than existing urban areas which would have subsequently been divided by a borderline (DORFMAN, 2009). The current degree of urbanisation of the border region between Brazil and Uruguay is in accordance with the strategic nature of this border: at 82%,[11] its degree of urbanisation index is the highest amongst Brazilian borderlands (BRASIL, 2009).

The urbanisation process was concluded during the period going from 1850 to 1909 (PALERMO, 2019), producing the series of twin border towns situated at the border which are still in existence in present days. From the west to the east, citing the Brazilian town followed by the Uruguayan town and the current name followed by the original name in parentheses, these are: Barra do Quaraí-Bella Unión (Santa Rosa del Cuareín), Quaraí-Artigas (San Eugenio), Santana do Livramento-Rivera (Villa de Ceballos), Aceguá-Aceguá, Jaguarão-Río Branco (Villa Artigas), and Chuí-Chuy. Historically, these cities

Cultural governance in the Brazil-Uruguay borderlands 47

developed in a context of weak road networks connecting them to the rest of their country, whilst being closely connected to the neighbouring twin city (MÜLLER, 2002).

In this research, we focused more specifically on the twin city conurbations of Santana do Livramento-Rivera and Jaguarão-Río Branco, situated as in Figure 4.6:

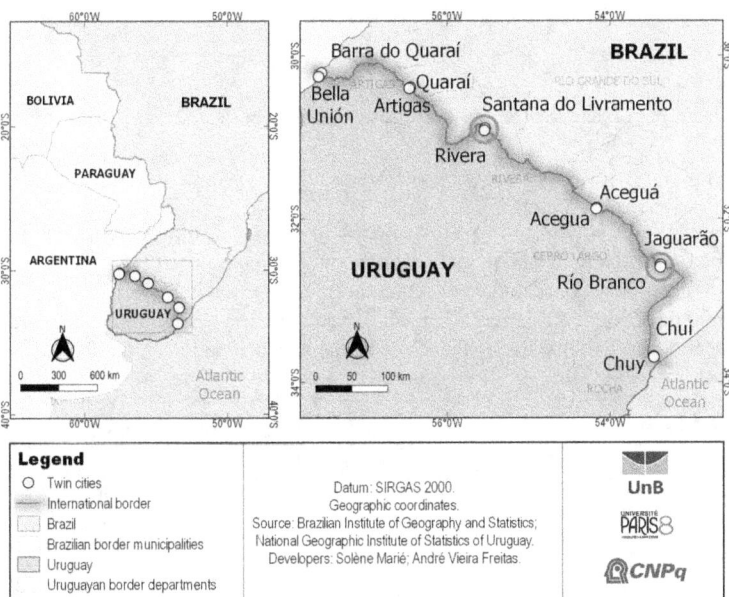

Figure 4.6 Santana do Livramento-Rivera, Jaguarão-Río Branco and other twin cities at the border between Brazil and Uruguay

Credit: André Vieira Freitas (cartography) and Solène Marié

The Brazilian city of Santana do Livramento was split from the municipality of Alegrete in 1857, gaining the status of village. The urbanisation process in the neighbouring Uruguayan city of Rivera was launched in the second half of the 19th century by the central Uruguayan government and the city was founded in 1862 (Figure 4.7). It was built for strategic reasons linked to the control of national territory and borders, against Brazilian expansion in the north of Uruguay (ASEFF, 2006). Nowadays, the city is the capital of the Uruguayan department of the same name and hosts 78,900 inhabitants.[12]

The association of the two cities, referred to by some inhabitants as "Riveramento" (junction of their two names), composes nowadays a single urban complex crossed by a dry international border which is dissimulated amongst

48 *Cultural governance in the Brazil-Uruguay borderlands*

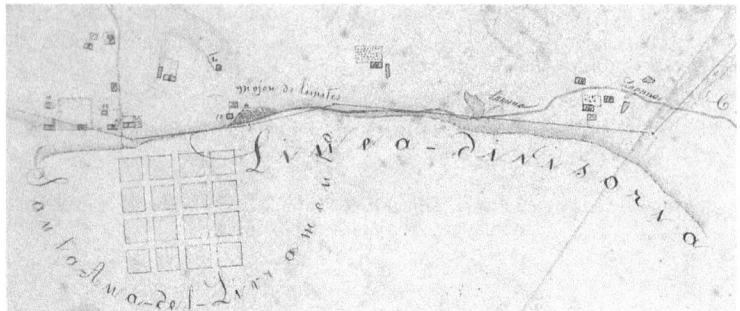

Figure 4.7 Urbanisation of Villa Ceballos (now Rivera) in 1865. Map by José Pompilio Lupi.

Copyright: Museo del Patrimonio Regional de Rivera

a mixture of streets and squares. Circulation is free within the conurbation, and the structure of the streets is similar and thus complementary.

A number of border marks such as the one displayed in Figure 4.8 are scattered throughout the conurbation, but they are not very perceptible due to their location in the outskirts of the cities or their incorporation in the landscape.

Figure 4.8 Brazil-Uruguay border mark in the conurbation of Santana do Livramento (Brazil) and Rivera (Uruguay)[13]

Credit: Solène Marié

Furthermore, these pyramidal stone structures do not explicitly mention the border or the two neighbouring nations: nothing is inscribed on them.

The Barón of Mauá International Bridge (Figure 4.9),[14] which connects Jaguarão (Brazil) to Río Branco (Uruguay), was built between 1927 and 1930 with Uruguayan funds based on a war debt of the latter towards Brazil and following a treaty signed between the two countries in June 1918. Prior to the construction of the bridge, daily exchanges of goods and people between the two border cities and regions had been performed by boat across the Jaguarão River since the 19th century (FRIZZO; RIBEIRO; DE ÁVILA; 2015). Nowadays, the bridge plays a physical role of easing the passage between the two cities, but its role goes further: "beyond this, it is the symbol of this border" (FRIZZO; RIBEIRO; DE ÁVILA, 2015, p. 282).

(a)   (b)

Figure 4.9 Barón of Mauá International bridge between the cities of Jaguarão and Río Branco viewed from the Brazilian (a) and Uruguayan (b) sides of the border

Credit: Solène Marié

Nowadays, the city of Jaguarão possesses a population of 28,393 inhabitants[15] and Río Branco of 14,600.[16]

As a region mainly dedicated to the activity of cattle breeding, the borderlands also constituted transit areas, used for transhumance and to gather supplies. The coexistence of border towns' role as pathways with their role as military posts demonstrates the tension between a search for and a control of contact between both sides of the border (DORFMAN, 2009).

4.3.2 Economic activity and networks in the borderlands

Beyond its historical and socio-demographic origins, the interaction between borderlanders always was and is still based on economic exchange. Borderlanders seek in the neighbouring territory that which is inaccessible in their own, creating a structure of mutual dependence in the exchanges of goods. Furthermore, the military posts which marked the history of the border region

50 *Cultural governance in the Brazil-Uruguay borderlands*

for reasons linked to territorial control also served an economic purpose: that of controlling the entrance of smuggled goods onto the territory, activity which took place throughout a large part of its history (CLEMENTE, 2010). Thus, life in these borderlands brought with it, for structural reasons, the establishment of economic exchanges (Figure 4.10).

(a) (b)

Figure 4.10 Marks of the border on shopfronts in Santana do Livramento (a) and Jaguarão (b)

Credit: Solène Marié

Beyond these structural reasons, economic activity was also led to cross the border for a number of other reasons. Firstly, smuggling as an everyday life practice is a historical feature of the region which persists to present days, as an exercise of economic rationality based on price variations in the two neighbouring countries (PALERMO, 2019; DORFMAN, 2009). Furthermore, for geographical and historical reasons and due to movements of populations and investments, interdependence developed in the region and resulted in cross-border production, sales and capital networks (CLEMENTE, 2010).

Economic growth in the decade of 1810 and territorial conflict led to the deepening of these networks, mainly around the production of salted meat. In Brazil, the first saladero[17] was founded in 1737 in Pelotas, Rio Grande do Sul, north of the border region. Progressive growth of the sector based on the use of salted meat to feed enslaved populations culminated towards the consolidation of the sector and what came to be known as the saladero cycle[18] from the beginning of the 20th century. From 1884, saladeros were also created in the border region, some of them by Uruguayans. According to Dorfman (2009), the location of these Uruguayan saladeros is closely linked to the presence of the border as constructing them in Brazilian territory enabled Uruguayans to get around tariffs and other trade barriers imposed by the Brazilian government. Alongside reasons linked to changes in eating habits, to the competition arising from refrigeration starting in the 1910s and to the abolition of slavery which eliminated the main producers and consumers of salted meat[19], their decline was also linked to protectionist laws issued under Getúlio Vargas's leadership. These aimed to restrict the transit of Brazilian product through the Uruguayan territory, to strengthen the links of the borderlands with the rest of Southern Brazil and coastal area and to restrict the employment of foreigners. One of the effects of these policies was to increase the pursuit for dual Uruguayan-Brazilian citizenship[20] (DORFMAN, 2009).

In the period going from 1870 to 1930, interdependence increased throughout the borderlands as a whole with the creation of deeper relations between economic actors (CLEMENTE, 2010). With the development of these joint companies and networks in the borderlands, a new type of businessperson came into existence: the "borderlander",[21] as designated by Jacob (2004).

The period also saw Uruguayan companies create Brazilian branches in Rio Grande do Sul[22] and make direct investments in the neighbouring territory. These activities were developed in sectors such as banking, telecommunications and the production of optical and medical equipment. They benefitted from the existence of a local workforce enabled by the free circulation of workers (JACOB, 2004).

Following a phase dominated by activities linked to agriculture, cattle breeding and the production of salted meat as highlighted previously, the subsequent one based on services and industrial goods was curbed by protectionist policies implemented in Brazil in the 1930s. Also, the construction of railway lines in the south of Brazil which connected better Rio Grande do Sul's economy with the Brazilian economic pole of São Paulo reverted the historical position of Montevideo as the most accessible port for Rio Grande do Sul's production, via railways which were in existence previously. This production came to subsequently travel via the port of Rio Grande in Brazil (CLEMENTE, 2010). A reversal of financial and economic flows was then noted, with the buying of land by Brazilians in the northern part of Uruguay from 1950.

4.3.3 People of the borderlands: the demographics

The demographics of the borderlands were influenced by the fact that they played the role of a "zone of friction and conflict between American reigns of Spain and Portugal" (HEREDIA, 1998, p. 121). Notably, whilst the town of Rivera was created as a barrier to Brazilian expansionism, its first censuses conducted in 1867 and 1895 show that within its inhabitants, the number of Brazilians surpassed the number of Uruguayans (DORFMAN, 2009).

At the end of the 19th century, as a result of what Artigas identified as an expansionist project from the Portuguese in the northern band of Uruguay (PALERMO, 2001), measures were taken in order to "orientalise" the region. One of the measures consisted in encouraging European immigration in order to reduce the proportion of Brazilian descendants in the population (DORFMAN, 2009).

52 Cultural governance in the Brazil-Uruguay borderlands

Beyond the influence of this friction between two powers and of European immigration, another factor which influences the composition of the local population is the presence of indigenous populations and of Afro-descendants. The former, under the names of Charrua, Guarani and Chanaé, were the first populations in the region, and through the Jesuit missions, their history was intimately linked to the territory between present-day Brazil, Argentina, Paraguay and neighbouring Uruguay.

The presence of Afro-descendant populations is linked to the industry of salted meat which was the main activity in the region at the beginning of the 20th century and was based on intense slave labour. The differentiated abolition of slavery in the two countries (in 1842 in Uruguay and in 1888 in Brazil) led to movements of black enslaved populations between the two countries, searching for recognition of citizenship (Figure 4.11).

Figure 4.11 Street in the border conurbation of Chuí (Brazil)-Chuy (Uruguay)
Credit: Solène Marié

This mosaic of populations has constituted today's borderlands which, despite the fact that they are situated in remote, peripheral areas and are composed of rural zones with small urban groupings, can be seen as constituting cosmopolitan societies.[23]

Cultural governance in the Brazil-Uruguay borderlands 53

4.3.4 People of the borderlands: cultural and linguistic features

In his work on cultural regionalisation in Uruguay, Felipe Arocena (2011) created a typology to classify the country's territory based on the similarity of socio-economic structures and cultural and linguistic characteristics. Based on the analysis of 28 indicators, he distinguished the following 7 cultural regions: Montevideo, Canelones, Centro, Suroeste, Litoral, Norte and Este.

Alongside Montevideo and Canelones which constitute independent cases by the sheer size of their population and thus are set aside from the rest of the country, he therefore distinguishes five other regions. The northern region groups departments which are characterised by a strong Brazilian influence from the point of view both of language and of exposition to Brazilian media, whilst the southwest region is defined by cultural influence from Buenos Aires in these same two aspects. The region named "Litoral" presents links to the Argentine states of Entre Ríos and Buenos Aires. The eastern region is characterised by the strong influence of tourism linked to its coastal location as well as by the differentiated level of development of its regional and cultural policies. Finally, the central region, composed of departments situated south of Río Negro, is characterised by the absence of borders and coastal areas (AROCENA, 2011). Amongst the departments which are situated along the borderline, three (Artigas, Rivera, Cerro Largo) are part of the northern region characterised by Brazilian influence and two (Treinta y Tres, Rocha) situated on the eastern part around the Mirim Lagoon belong to the grouping of the eastern set of departments under the influence of the coast.

One of the most visible signs of cultural differentiation in these borderlands is its expression in language. José Pedro Varela, Uruguayan intellectual, wrote in 1876 regarding the north of the country "in all this zone even the national language has already been lost, as Portuguese is the language which is most commonly spoken" (apud PALERMO, 2019, p. 21). Until the end of the 19th century could be encountered on Uruguayan territory areas in which the Guarani, Portuguese, Portuñol,[24] Basque, French and Italian languages were spoken. Varela's 1877 Education Law, designed with the aim of fostering national unity and identity based on the exclusive use of the Spanish language in schools, prohibited the use of other languages. The only languages for which registers can be found beyond the beginning of the 20th century are Portuguese and Portuñol, which continued to be used by a large portion of the population in the borderlands. According to Palermo (2019), this is linked to the fact that both were lingua franca in the borderlands, with support from dominant social sectors.

The presence of the Portuguese language in northern Uruguay was one element of Brazilian cultural influence in the region and played a part in the development of Portunhol/Portuñol.[25] This linguistic phenomenon has been referred to as *Fronterizo, Mixtura, Brasilero, Entreverado, Portugués del Uruguay (PU)* or *Portuñol Riverense*, these names being used alternatively to designate the phenomenon. These names could be translated to English as follows: Borderlandian, Mix, Brasilian, Mixed up, Uruguayan Portuguese or Portuñol from Rivera. It is referred to by some academics as DPU[26]: Uruguayan Portuguese Dialects (ELIZAINCÍN; BEHARES; BARRIOS, 1987). Other linguists prefer to consider portuñol within the scope of languages rather than that of dialects in order to consider fully its historical construction and relevance (STURZA, 2019). Given the various forms of Portuñol which can be encountered in the different locations where it is spoken (MÜLLER, 2002), mainly in the border twin cities, many argue that the language should be referred to in the plural form: portuñoles/portunhóis.[27]

Beyond the various denominations which are used to describe the phenomenon of portuñol, a number of different forms can be distinguished. Sturza (2019) distinguishes four of them: Portuñol as an interlanguage (the transition between the beginner and proficient use of the language); Portuñol Uruguaio (used as an ethnic, contact language spoken in the north of Uruguay as an inheritance of historical and cultural contact with luso-Brazilians); Portuñol for communicative interaction (used in the informal context of everyday relations); *Portuñol Salvaje*, which could be translated as Wild or Free Portuñol (linguistic resource used for aesthetic and political purposes, mostly used in literary texts).

This culture of the borderlands encounters an expression in literature, for example in the works of writers such as Aldyr Garcia Schlee,[28] born in Jaguarão and main literary figure of the border. Other 20th-century writers such as Cyro Martins, Simões Lopes Netto, Alcides Maya, Amaro Juvenal or Aureliano Figueiredo Pinto are representative of a literature which can generally be said to be an expression of the culture of the La Plata region (MASINA, 2002). The latter constitutes an interstitial space between various national and linguistic territories, linked to a social interpenetration enabled by the pampa which creates similarities in terms of subjects and vocabulary (ROCCA, 2002) as well as a particular relation to orality and the mixing of languages (CHIAPPINI, 2002).

Panitz (2015, 2016) argues that there exists a shared cultural space in the La Plata region, involving Argentina, Uruguay and Brazil and which expresses itself through musical networks. The latter can be identified between the cities of Buenos Aires (Argentina), Montevideo (Uruguay), Pelotas and Porto Alegre (Brazil).

The musical genre produced by these artists combines elements of folklore, folk and pop music. It is based on identitarian elements which can be found in the three countries' shared culture, and its networks in turn contribute to cultural integration processes in the La Plata region. Artists such as Vitor Ramil, Jorge and Daniel Drexler or Richard Serraria, through their work and discourses, contribute to the production of representations on their region:

> These artists' music is rooted in the La Plata region, which is mostly represented by the pampa landscape. The characteristics which are put forth to identify this shared space allude to its rhythms, its cross-border aspect,

the history of this zone, the contiguity of the pampa, the climate, the occurrence of a period of economic and cultural integration.

(PANITZ, 2015, p. 12)

Secondly, these representations are the basis for practices which, through the creation of events and collaboration networks, influence existing musical space.

The borderlands also have an expression in visual arts. Amongst artists who have worked across the border, Osmar Santos is a particularly important figure both artistically and in terms of artistic leadership and training for subsequent generations.[29]

The presentation of different aspects of shared culture which can be encountered in these borderlands, though not intending to be exhaustive, served to demonstrate the existence of a strong cultural convergence linked to a number of geographic, historic and demographic factors presented previously. Undubitatively, this convergence is present and visible in the borderlands, especially in urban areas. However, some scholars question whether these relations can definitely be considered to constitute integration (MÜLLER, 2002). Others warn against the fact that some scholars

> share a unifying, romantic idea: in principle, these cities [...] symbol of the peace between two nations, share common social spaces which are devoid of conflict and ethnic differences.
>
> (ASEFF, 2006, pp. 18–19)

However, as pointed out in Section 2.1.3, border regions combine converging and diverging dynamics, and, whilst everyday interaction favours contact and thus alikeness, it also often generates an increase in frictions and conflict (GRIMSON, 2000). According to Grimson, inhabitants of many border regions are bearers of a discourse around the inexistence of the border and of an integration between populations, but it is problematic if researchers reproduce this discourse and thus do not see that the border "is inexistent for some things and existent for others" (GRIMSON, 2000, p. 149)."

4.4 Cultural governance in the borderlands: institutional context and cooperation

As pointed out previously, by their very nature, borderlands are affected by phenomena of local, regional, national and international levels. Also, from the point of view of public policy, they necessarily need to be studied within a multi-level governance framework in order to take into account the policies from various sources which impact them. The institutional frameworks which will be presented subsequently therefore relate to various levels, and we will start with the highest level of governance.

4.4.1 Contribution of Mercosur to cultural governance in the borderlands

The study of the place given to culture in the agenda of the Southern Common Market (Mercosur) reveals that over the years, a gap between discourse and practice became evident. Despite multiple meetings, acts and initiatives, the practical results of the programmes put into operation are still incipient (BORJA, 2011).

An analysis of the way in which the topic was brought about by Mercosur's different instances indicates at least two distinct phases. The first, which ran from 1992 to 2003, was marked by the creation of advisory bodies and by the establishment of the founding principles for the cultural dimension of Mercosur's interventions.

The Treaty of Asunción, Mercosur's founding document signed in 1991, did not mention the theme of culture in its core. In spite of this the first discussions within the bloc on the role that culture would play in the Member States' integration process were held the following year, in 1992. On the same year was created the Mercosur's Specialized Meeting on Culture,[30] the first forum for culture-related discussions in the bloc. Although its creation took place in 1992, its first meeting was only held in 1995, three years later.

In 1995, after the signing of the Memorandum of Understanding considered the first document exclusively dedicated to the topic of culture within the scope of the bloc, a forum for the discussion and articulation of state bureaucracies related to culture was created under the name of Mercosur Cultural (BORJA, 2011). The lack of assertiveness (or effectiveness) of Mercosur Cultural in its ability to implement projects makes authors refer to this instance as a "mere abstraction, an agency which only deals with generalities and merely ratifies, praises or repeats that the bloc's countries must support cultural projects in the region" (CHIAPPINI, 2011, p. 6).

The Meeting of Ministers of Culture (RMC[31]) was created as a forum for negotiations between cultural policymakers from the different Member States (BIJOS; ARRUDA, 2010), but although a significant number of projects were discussed, none were actually implemented (BORJA, 2011).

Finally, in 1996 were created the Mercosur's Cultural Integration Protocol[32] and its Cultural Parliament (PARCUM[33]). The aim of the latter was to harmonise Member States' cultural legislations (BIJOS; ARRUDA, 2010).

The second phase, which began in 2003, was marked by continuity in terms of consultative meetings but also by the implementation, albeit in a disjointed way, of Mercosur's first cultural programmes.

Implemented in 2009, the Mercosur Cultural Information System (SICSUR[34]) constitutes a digital platform for the production and reproduction of cultural sector data in all the bloc's Member States as well as in Chile, Ecuador and Colombia. The platform displays maps of cultural activities, statistics and research produced on the topic. The idea had arisen in 1996, during the elaboration of Mercosur's Cultural Integration Protocol, but it had not been put into practice until then. The platform remained active until 2016 but was not accessible during the elaboration of this book.

The Mercosur Audiovisual Programme[35] stems from the creation of the Specialized Meeting of Mercosur Cinematographic and Audiovisual Authorities (RECAM), in 2003. As a "Specialized Meeting", this initiative is not within the scope of Mercosur Cultural.

The Mercosur Cultural Fund,[36] created to fund joint cultural programmes within the bloc, was officialised in 2003. However, it is still inoperative as it has not yet been regulated by the Member States. In Brazil, the decree for its creation was only submitted in 2015 and to date, it is still in process.[37]

Despite the ineffectiveness of the projects and programmes presented since the creation of Mercosur, it is possible to delineate the common guiding principles of the policies implemented so far: the recognition of cultural diversity as inherent in the Member States' populations and the internalisation of this element as essential for the elaboration of public policies aimed at regional integration; the understanding of culture as a resource and a tool for the consolidation of the integration process; and the recognition of the importance of the cultural economy for member and associated states (BORJA, 2011).

The explanations for the low effectiveness of Mercosur cultural programmes are diverse. For Soares (2008), Mercosur countries have not historically and individually developed a cultural diplomacy to complement their traditional diplomatic activity. Therefore, there is a predominance of strategies based on the exercise of *hard power* rather than *soft power* in the bloc, and culture is not seen as a supporting factor in the foreign policy implemented by its Member States. Generally, within Mercosur initiatives, there is a prevalence of commercial issues over cultural, political and social ones (DE SOUZA, 2004; MINEIRO, 2000; SOARES, 2008), as Figure 4.12 humorously illustrates.

Analysing Mercosur's cultural integration process, as mentioned earlier, it is possible to say that the bloc is in its embryonic phase (MARTINS, 2007) marked by sparse and discontinued initiatives. It can also be argued that, similarly to the European integration process, the integration sought by Mercosur creators was not necessarily cultural integration: the focus was always much more directed towards economic and commercial issues (BORJA, 2011). So much so that, as mentioned, the term "culture" does not appear in the Treaty of Asunción, which constituted the bloc.

The little importance given to culture as a necessary element in the integration process can also possibly be attributed to the idea that Southern countries should not invest in cultural policies at a time when their efforts should be directed towards policies focusing on economic and social development (FERREIRA, 2012).

Regarding Mercosur's contribution to issues related to the borderlands between its Member states, a few elements can be highlighted. Firstly, despite the fact that Brazil shares borders with all other Mercosur member countries, the

Figure 4.12 Shop in Santana do Livramento, "Mercosul Shoes"
Credit: Solène Marié

initiatives geared towards integration in the borderlands are based on bilateral and not on multilateral agreements (SOARES, 2008; CARNEIRO FILHO; LEMOS, 2014). The only two initiatives linked to borderlands within the scope of the Mercosur are its Fund for the Structural Convergence and Strengthening of the Institutional Structure (FOCEM[38]) and the Ad Hoc Group on Borderland Integration (GAHIF[39]), which corresponds to bilateral actions developed within the bloc on the issue of cooperation in the borderlands. However, Mercosur does not possess any specific forums or multilateral policies for its borderlands.

In this sense, the Mercosur follows a different orientation from that of the European Union, which followed the "strategic objective of overcoming or coordinating differences, which is articulated as a supranational ideology" (MARTINS, 2007, p. 92). However, it does offer a variable degree of support to bilateral initiatives and generally contributes to the creation of a cooperative environment between member countries, which promotes the opening of borders (CARNEIRO FILHO; LEMOS, 2014).

Furthermore, a role of symbolic recognition of borderland initiatives can be attributed to Mercosur, as well as one of increasing self-esteem and conscience of borderland dynamics amongst local population. In 2009, the municipality of Santana do Livramento received Brazilian federal recognition as the symbol of Brazilian integration with other Mercosur countries.[40] This gesture is cited by cultural activists and local administration agents as having brought attention to the existence of specific cultural dynamics between Santana do Livramento and Rivera. Also, though it was a federal and not a Mercosur-led initiative, for the local population, it created a connection to the Mercosur which generated attention and self-esteem.[41]

In the border twin cities of Jaguarão and Río Branco, it is the Barón of Mauá International Bridge which connects the two cities that received similar recognition from Mercosur. The bridge was listed as a national historical monument by Uruguay in 1977 and was in 2011 the first binational monument to be listed as national historical monument by Brazil's National Institute of Historic and Artistic Heritage (IPHAN[42]). It was subsequently listed by Mercosur Cultural as the Mercosur's first historical monument.

4.1.2 Contribution of the Federal State to cultural governance in the borderlands

Regarding the influence of State policies and politics on the border region, the first element which comes to mind is naturally the existence of border strips on both sides of the Brazil-Uruguay borderline. In the case of Brazil, country which currently has the widest border strip in the subcontinent (CARNEIRO; CAMARA, 2019), the border strip is the result of a long historical process which goes back to colonial times. Its width was initially of ten leagues (66 km), and it was modified in 1934, 1937 and 1946. The current legal framework[43] determines the existence of a 150-kilometer wide strip of territory along the borderline which is regulated through specific rules (MOREIRA et al., 2008; LOSADA; SADECK, 2015) in terms of transit, spatial occupation and economic exploitation. The administrative body which is in charge of the application of these rules in the border strip is the National Defence Council (CDN[44]) (LOSADA; SADECK, 2015). A common confusion amongst border scholars is to assimilate the border strip with the National Security Strip[45] created through the Federal Constitution of 1934 in order to prevent the buying of land without approval from the National Superior Security Council.[46] Initially wider than the border strip in its previous dimensions, the latter came to cover the same area as the border strip (CARNEIRO; CAMARA, 2019).

The Brazilian border strip covers an area of approximately 2.3 million square kilometres (MOREIRA et al., 2008). This represents almost 27% of the national territory, ten million of its inhabitants (BRASIL, 2011), 588 municipalities (BRASIL, 2005) and thus 10% of Brazilian cities. Amongst these 588 border municipalities, the Southern region possesses the largest number with a total of 418, distributed as follows: Rio Grande do Sul (197), Paraná (139) and Santa Catarina (82) (LOSADA; SADECK, 2015).

Brazilian borders are highly heterogeneous, with large municipalities[47] in the northern part of the border and therefore a higher proportion of non-bordering municipalities with headquarters outside the border strip, and smaller municipalities and a larger number of twin cities in the southern part of the border (BRASIL, 2005).

Based on this diversity and the argument that the rules affecting different parts of the border strip should therefore be more individualised,[48] a bill was submitted by Carlos Bezerra[49] at the beginning of 2019[50] with the aim of maintaining the current width of the strip only in the Amazonian states of Amapá, Amazonas, Pará and Roraima. It would be reduced to 50 km in Rondônia, to 20 km in Mato Grosso and Mato Grosso do Sul and to 10 km in Rio Grande do Sul, Santa Catarina and Paraná. However, this bill is still in discussion, and therefore, the legal framework presented previously is the one currently in force. This is not the first initiative of the kind: between 2003 and 2014, a total of nine different bills were submitted with the same intention of reducing the size of the border strip and none of them were successful (MARIÉ, 2017a).

An analysis of the debate around the theme of borders in the national congress between 1990[51] and 2016 (MARIÉ, 2017a) brought about the following conclusions:

Firstly, three phases were distinguished in terms of the number of bills submitted on the topic of borders within the National Congress: (1) from 1990 to 1998, very few bills were submitted on the topic; (2) from 1999 to 2009, there was a sharp and significant increase in the number of bills and (3) from 2010 to 2016, the topic lost space in the legislature, with a lower number of bills than in the previous period.

Secondly, an analysis of the border-related issues addressed in the bills over the period brings about the following conclusions: in the first decade of the period under study (from 1990 to 1999), bills focused on an average number of topics and focused mainly on the establishment of the legal framework for borders. There was also a sudden and strong increase in the number of bills submitted in 1999. In the second decade (from 2000 to 2010), there was a strong increase in the attention given to the topic. Furthermore, though administrative matters and land policy did not disappear from the agenda, they lost space to the issues of economic and regional development, which entered the agenda from 2007. There was also a strong focus on the issue of reducing the size of the border strip which was the subject of several bills, as well as a peak in the number of bills submitted in 2008, the highest within the period. Finally, in the third decade (from 2010 to 2016), there was a decline in issues linked to agricultural and regional development and an increase in those linked to economic and regional development suggesting that regional development moved from being linked to agricultural issues to economic issues. Despite this transition to issues of economic development, it is worth noting that issues of security and land policy remained on the agenda despite the introduction of new themes (BRASIL, 2013; MARIÉ, 2017a).

Figure 4.13 summarises the collected data and resulting analysis:

Cultural governance in the Brazil-Uruguay borderlands 61

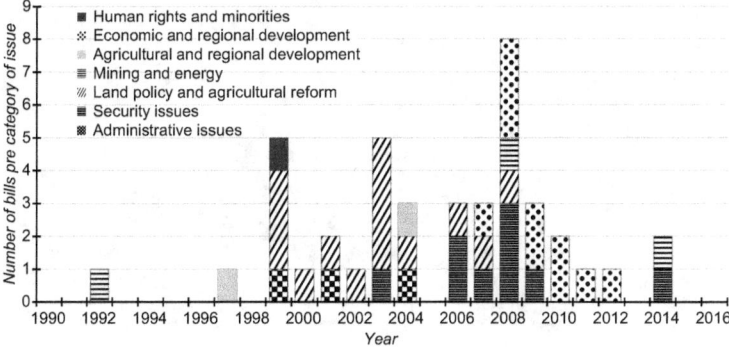

Figure 4.13 Evolution of the number of bills and of the border-related issues covered
Credit: Adapted and translated from MARIÉ, 2017a

Finally, the analysis of the actors involved in these legislative processes points to a prevalence of Congresspeople from the Southern region in the submission of bills on this topic: they are responsible for 53% of the bills submitted in the period.[52] The State of Rio Grande do Sul alone is responsible for 35% of the bills, whilst the percentage of Congresspeople from this state is of 6%. Despite this, the overrepresentation of the South does not appear in terms of bills designed for a specific region: 86% of the bills apply to the entire national territory. However, this demonstrates the involvement and influence on the agenda that Brazil's Southern region has in terms of border issues (MARIÉ, 2017a).

The year of 2002 was a landmark for borderland integration between Brazil and Uruguay when State action on a bilateral level led to an important initiative which is worth highlighting: in that year, the two countries established a programme of binational cooperation and integration based on the demands of borderlanders (FURTADO, 2013; LEMOS; RÜCKERT, 2014). The New Agenda for Borderland Cooperation and Development between Brazil and Uruguay[53] included seven activity areas: health, education and vocational training, sanitation and environment, political and judicial cooperation, social policies, labour issues and areas of integrated control (CARNEIRO FILHO; LEMOS, 2014). It also created a Borderland Integration Zone[54] through the Agreement Granting Residence, Academic and Work Permission to Borderland Brazilian and Uruguayan Nationals.[55] This agreement was formalised through Decree nº 5,105 of 2004 and established an area of 20 km in which both countries grant benefits to resident communities, considered borderlanders (FURTADO, 2013) (Figure 4.14).

Another important landmark is 2010 when, following the election of President José Mujica in Uruguay, various binational encounters were organised

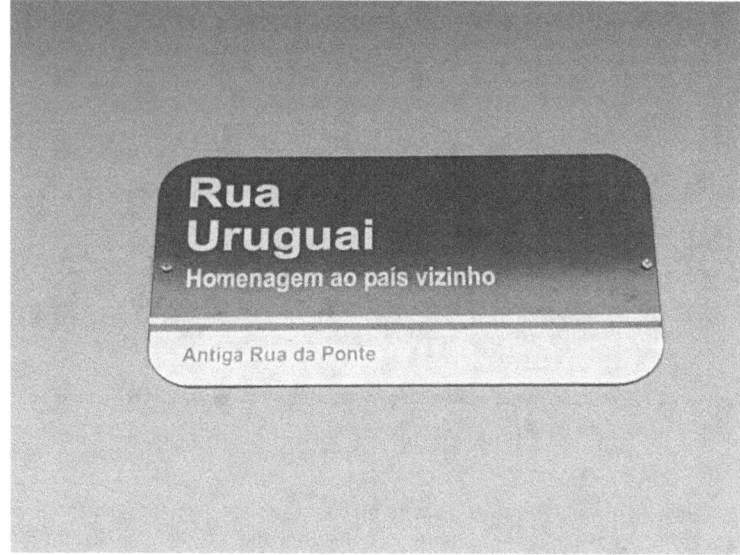

Figure 4.14 "Bridge Street" in Jaguarão, renamed "Uruguay Street" in honour of the neighbouring country

Credit: Solène Marié

with President Luiz Inácio Lula da Silva based on similar visions and fluid communication between the two leaders. An encounter in Brasília on the 29th of March, followed by another one on the 4th of May in Montevideo, and a last encounter in Santana do Livramento in July led to the signature of four agreements on the 30th of July 2010 (CLEMENTE, 2010). The latter covered general bilateral issues as well as specific issues affecting borderlanders. However, none of these agreements touched upon culture-related issues.

Finally, a general contribution of state action to integration in the borderlands which is highlighted is that of the reduction of bureaucratic constraints (bureaucratic obstacles as well as paperwork) and the creation of infrastructure. Bento (2015b) argues that the local integration process is more intense in conurbated border twin cities than in border twin cities which are separated by a geographic obstacle, for example by a river. This is due to two factors: lower levels of interaction due to the obstacle which physically reduces fluxes and the fact that, whilst in the first group of cities border controls tend to be shifted to the outskirts of the conurbation (as in Santana do Livramento-Rivera, for example), in the second one there are national border controls situated at the obstacle (as in Jaguarão-Río Branco, at the two ends of the Baron of Mauá bridge, for example). Whilst the creation of infrastructure does not address the second factor, it reduces the first factor by easing fluxes between the two municipalities.

Cultural governance in the Brazil-Uruguay borderlands 63

In terms of Brazilian Federal programmes geared towards the border region, a number of consecutive initiatives were led from 1954 to 2019, with frequent changes in names and governance structures of the programmes. A concise chronology of the latter is presented in Table 4.1, along with the main actions and their impact.

Table 4.1 Concise chronology of federal instruments for border governance, their content and impact

Year	Name of implemented programme	Leading institution	Actions and impact
1955 (institutionalised in 1979)	Financial assistance programme for Border Strip Municipalities[56]	Secretaria de Assuntos Estratégicos (Presidência da República)	Very limited impact
1999	Border Strip Social Programme[57]	Secretaria de Desenvolvimento Regional (Ministério da Integração Nacional)	Investment in urban infrastructure and small construction work. Very few regions received support
2003	Border Strip Development programme[58] (PDFF) *Name subsequently modified to*: Border Strip Development Promotion Programme[59] (PDFF)	Secretaria de Programas Regionais (Ministério da Integração Nacional)	- Conceptual reformulation of border-related notions - Division of Brazilian borders into sections and sub-regions - Actions based on twin border cities and local cross-border economy
2005	Restructuring Proposal for the Border Strip Development programme[60] (PDFF)	Grupo Retis/Federal University of Rio de Janeiro	
2008	Foundations for a Border Strip Development and Integration Proposal[61]	Grupo de Trabalho Interfederativo de Integração Fronteiriça (GTI)	Introduction of a new governance model, based on the collaboration of border-related actors and institutions on various levels within the Permanent Commission for Border Strip Development and Integration[62] (CDIF)
2010		Comissão Permanente para o Desenvolvimento e a Integração da Faixa de Fronteira (CDIF)	Lack of coordination, especially from the State Border Nuclei,[63] in charge of the articulation between local and federal institutions
2017	*Name subsequently modified to*: Border Strip Development and Integration Plans[64]		

Credit: Solène Marié

It is worth noting the inexistence of a structured and up-to-date database on border issues in any Brazilian institution in order to centralise the information (CARNEIRO; CAMARA, 2019). This demonstrates a disconnection between the central federal government and border issues as well as a discontinuity in its actions, and generates a difficulty in studying these issues.

Detail regarding the programmes will not be given for the majority of them, given their discontinuity and lack of effectiveness in impacting change in the borderlands (CARNEIRO; CAMARA, 2019).

However, Scherma (2015) and Da Silva and Caldeirão (2018) highlight the fact that during the Lula da Silva mandates as president of Brazil and through the PDFF, new aspects of border issues and understandings of the borderlands which were inexistent beforehand emerged in the relevant public policies (CARNEIRO; CAMARA, 2019).

Along with the opening of border policies to issues of integration, the Brazilian Federal Government launched a specific programme for the development of the border strip[65] in 2004. After some reforms, it was transformed into the Permanent Commission for the Development of the Border Strip,[66] in charge of managing actions in these zones along three lines: border security, economic and social development, and borderland cooperation and integration). As mentioned in Table 4.1, the PDFF based its actions on two elements: the strategic role of the border twin cities and the development of local cross-border economies (BRASIL, 2005, 2013).

A comparison of the amounts invested in the PDFF and those actually spent between 2006 and 2013 shows significant discrepancy between the amounts allocated to the programme and those actually distributed throughout the whole period. Between 2006 and 2011, the allocated amount totalled R$ 923,000,000. The amount which was actually paid totalled only R$ 70,178,999, therefore 7.6% of the amount initially dedicated to the programme (MONTEIRO, 2014 apud. CARNEIRO; CAMARA, 2019). This denotes a difficulty in the execution of the planned actions.

A study elaborated by Da Silva[67] and Caldeirão (2018) analyses the impact of the federal-level PDFF programme on public policies linked to tourism in the city of Jaguarão (including culture and heritage). Amongst the total of 59 actions included in programmes geared towards the sub-region called "Border of the Southern half of Rio Grande do Sul"[68] in which the municipality of Jaguarão is situated, 3 are linked to culture and heritage (thus, 5% of the programmes):

1 Support to the Calaguá Festival (Santa Vitória do Palmar) and to the Binational Bookfairs in Santana do Livramento and Jaguarão (Programme 1: Implementation of a cultural programme at the border);
2 Border cinema festival[69] in Bagé, Jaguarão and Chuy carnivals, and America and Pampa (Programme 1: Implementation of a cultural programme at the border);

3 Preservation and revitalisation of the tangible and intangible heritage (Programme 3: Historical and cultural heritage).

An analysis (DA SILVA, CALDEIRÃO, 2018) of the amounts raised by Jaguarão townhall for the programme, those thereafter actually committed and those ultimately paid by Jaguarão Cultural Department between 2014 and 2017 reveals a significant discrepancy between the amounts. From the budget raised by the townhall, between 2.56% and 8.04% (throughout the years) were thereafter committed to being spent by Jaguarão Cultural Department, and between 2.49% and 7.57% were actually spent. 2016 was the year with the lowest percentages, whilst 2015 demonstrates the highest percentages: of the R$64,183,195.69 raised, R$5,161,768.49 were committed (8.04%) and R$4,856,290.13 were paid (7.57%).

In semi-structured interviews, local employees[70] were asked about the National Regional Development Policy,[71] the PDFF and the Border Strip Development and Integration Plans. Only one employee indicated that he knew the National Regional Development Policy and the PDFF. No employee knew the Border Strip Development and Integration Plans.

Da Silva and Caldeirão (2018, p. 19) assess that

> Despite the fact that all the participants visualize actions from the PDFF in their day-to-day work, none of them received any type of training or presentation in order for them to work in line with federal legislation and 67% of the interviewees recognise the actions within Jaguarão townhall's budget, but as a local activity and with no connection to other levels of government.

This denotes a lack of awareness of funding processes and sources, as well as a possible lack of general training. Furthermore, it demonstrates a very clear disconnection of municipal personnel from federal programmes destined to them, possibly because of the lack of communication and training from the levels of government responsible for the elaboration of these plans. The authors of the study attribute the discontinuity of plans at municipal level to the lack of preparation and training of the personnel (both contract workers and civil servants), even though they are the individuals who both implement these programmes and benefit from them as borderlanders.

This discrepancy between the establishment of a federal framework for public policy in borderlands and its actual application is expressed clearly by Britos[72] (2018), President of Jaguarão Cultural Municipal Council[73]:

> On the one hand there are policies in place, we have the border policy and rights, the Ministry of Foreign Affairs the cross- border cultural policies. [...]
> "No crossing the bridge without the Ministry's authorisation in Montevideo"

"But wait, you told me there was a law of border policies [...] You talk about twin cities."

"I don't think we're there yet, don't think about it"

Well, people who come from Uruguay to participate in events here get to the bridge and to cross it it's a whole bureaucracy for them [...] So they get annoyed and they carry their instrument across the border [...] Border policies are pointless because they aren't applied. They debate and talk for nothing because people end up crossing the bridge on foot anyway.

According to an employee from the Brazilian Federal Revenue service at the border,[74] the problem is twofold. Firstly, there is a lack of knowledge regarding procedures which enable the crossing of the border in the context of cultural events. Secondly, these procedures are so complicated that only large organisations are able to carry them out.

Following this analysis of federal policies geared towards the borderlands, we will explore how international cultural policies and programmes developed by the Federal State have had an impact on the Brazil-Uruguay border region.

Until 2008, the institution which had authority and legitimacy in terms of cultural diplomacy in Brazil was the Ministry of Foreign Affairs (MRE),[75] more specifically its Cultural Department.[76] The Ministry of Culture (MinC) occasionally gave support to the MRE, but cultural diplomacy was not conceptualised from the MinC, and there were no lines for international activities within the latter's budget (MARIÉ, 2017b).

During Fernando Henrique Cardoso's mandate as president, from 1995 to 2002, Brazilian cultural diplomacy actions are identified as having been underpinned by the following five lines of action: (1) cultural funding based on tax waivers to companies, (2) action within international forums and based on cultural cooperation mechanisms, (3) monopoly of the MRE in elaborating and managing Brazilian cultural diplomacy, (4) incipient funding to the MRE's Cultural Department and (5) focus on actions aimed at linguistic exchange and archives (MARIÉ, 2017b).

Table 4.2 details the cultural and educational cooperation agreements signed by the MRE during the Cardoso mandate as well as the names of the partner countries. Amongst the 15 partners, 3 are neighbouring countries (Argentina, Bolivia and Venezuela), but Uruguay is not included. Only the agreement with Argentina brings about the topic of integration.

During the Luiz Inácio Lula da Silva mandates (2003–2010), cultural diplomacy actions were underpinned by the following five lines of action: (1) definition of a national project for Brazilian culture at the beginning of the first term, (2) diversification of the bodies engaged in cultural diplomacy actions, (3) positioning in favour of cultural diversity within international organisations, (4) expansion of the range of partner countries and (5) expansion of State investments in the apparatus dedicated to cultural diplomacy (MARIÉ, 2017b).

Table 4.2 List of cultural, technical and educational cooperation agreements signed during the Cardoso mandate (1995–2002)

1995	1996	1997	1998	1999	2000	2001	2002
Canada (audiovisual coproduction)	**South Africa** (co-operation in the cultural sector)	**Italy** (cultural cooperation)		**Peru** (cultural exchange for the re-passing of information in the sectors of radio and television)	**Costa Rica** (cultural exchange for the re-passing of information in the sectors of radio and television)	**Portugal** (agreement with the Camões Institute)	
Namibia (cultural and educational cooperation)		**Syria** (co-operation in the sectors of education, higher education and culture)		**Bolivia** (cultural cooperation)	**Venezuela** (cultural exchange for the re-passing of information in the sectors of radio, television and news agencies)		
Turkey (cultural and educational cooperation)		**Jamaica** (cultural and educational cooperation)			**Portugal** (friendship, cooperation and inquiries)		
		Argentina (cultural integration)			**Estonia** (cultural and educational cooperation)		
		Russia (cultural and educational cooperation)					

Credit: Reproduced and translated from MARIÉ, 2017b

In terms of partner countries, cultural diplomacy tendencies followed the general foreign policy orientation, with a diversification of partners alongside traditional ones, mainly the BRICS* and South and Latin American neighbours (BRASIL, 2010; BIJOS; ARRUDA, 2010). However, the main programmes identified within cultural diplomacy action do not include projects linked to Uruguay and its border with Brazil (MARIÉ, 2017b).

The main element which is worth highlighting from this administration is the gradual collaboration of the MRE and the MinC in terms of international projection of Brazilian culture (BRASIL, 2006; BARÃO, 2012; BIJOS; ARRUDA, 2010). The MinC left its advisory role to the MRE, and cultural diplomacy was redesigned to be thought of as a joint responsibility of both ministries (MARIÉ, 2017b). For the organisation of the Year of Brazil in France (2005) and of the Year of France in Brazil (2009)[77], the first large events of the sort, the MinC created in 2007 a Committee for the Internationalisation of Brazilian Culture,[78] which was then transformed into what became the Board of International Relations (DRI[79]) in 2008. The decree through which the committee was created demonstrates the actual opening of the policy of cultural diplomacy to the MinC, including the following responsibilities: extend Brazilian foreign policy guidelines in the area of culture; ensure their adoption in the international cultural actions of the Ministry and related entities; outline strategies and support actions for the intensification of cultural exchange between Brazil and foreign countries, in articulation with the other areas of the Ministry.

The official involvement of the MinC in international actions, thus the sharing of cultural diplomacy actions between the MRE and sectorial specialists in cultural policy, made a difference which appears to be key in the development of networks with actors in the Brazil-Uruguay border region.

Beyond the possible positive bias that populations may have towards artists and intellectuals rather than politicians, the existence of a negative bias towards federal politics associated with the distant capital is very present in the Brazil-Uruguay borderlands, for reasons linked to the regionalisation of politics and the perception of federal policies as being ill-suited to local reality.

Thus, we are led to think that amongst the policies emanating from the Federal State, cultural policies have a higher propensity to be perceived and received positively in the borderlands than other types of policies, even if the latter are designed specifically for the borderlands.

In the study conducted by Da Silva and Caldeirão (2018), in the answers of municipal personnel to questions relating to the knowledge of federal policies for the borderlands, staff from the Planning and Urbanism Secretary were those who demonstrated the highest degree of knowledge of programmes in relation to other employees. They were able to present detailed information about Jaguarão's participation in the federal Growth

---

* Group of States initially comprising Brazil, Russia, India and China, joined by South Africa in 2011 and Saudi Arabia, Egypt, the United Arab Emirates, Ethiopia and Iran in 2024

Acceleration Programme (PAC[80]) for Historical Cities, since 2009, with a budget of R$40,000,000 for the renovation of historical buildings.

The PAC for Historical Cities was launched in 2009 as a special line of action within the PAC, a federal programme of economic policies launched in 2007 in order to boost Brazilian economic growth based on investment in infrastructure. Specifically, it was a collaboration of the federal government with the Brazilian National Institute of Historic and Artistic Heritage (IPHAN[81]). The funding was redistributed by the Ministries of Culture, Education and Tourism to 173 cities which already possessed listed historical monument or were in process of being listed. The involvement of two institutions linked to cultural policies in this programme may have contributed to them being better assimilated by borderlands municipal personnel.

Similarly, whilst none of the 22 border city personnel or activists interviewed during the course of this research referred to the PDFF in the interviews, frequent mentions were made to Juca Ferreira[82] visiting the borderlands as Minister of Culture. On the 30th of May 2015, on the occasion of the recognition of the Barón of Mauá bridge as Mercosul cultural heritage, the "Border Dialogue"[83] event was organised. Alongside public authorities from the cultural sector in Brazil and Uruguay such as Maria Julia Muñoz, Uruguayan Minister of Education and Culture and Jurema Machado, President of the Brazilian IPHAN, it attracted to the town of Jaguarão university professors, cultural activists and artists from other parts of the Uruguayan department of Cerro Largo and the Brazilian state of Rio Grande do Sul and even from other Brazilian states (COMUNELLO, 2018).

Though it may seem contradictory, these various facts lead us to think that in terms of federal authorities and policies originating from Brasília, those relating to the cultural sector have a higher ability to reach the borderlands than those relating to borderlands.

4.1.3 Contribution of the Rio Grande do Sul state to cultural governance in the borderlands

Brazil's 1988 constitution, which prevails currently, does not institutionalise paradiplomacy. However, there is no specific rule prohibiting sub-national governments from acting internationally. Furthermore, a number of specific responsibilities are handed over to them by the federal government (MILANI; RIBERO, 2011), and the central state recognises a number of decentralised cooperation networks, such as Mercocidades, a cooperation network of cities within the framework of the Mercosul. Nevertheless, officially, all international actions remain a prerogative of the central state, as established in article 21 of the constitution: "Is a prerogative of the Federal State: I – to maintain relations with foreign States and take part in international organisations", and thus, Brazilian paradiplomacy is maintained within "unlawful practices" (VIGEVANI, 2006, p. 131).

The consequences of this legal-institutional framework are multiple. Firstly, the result is not an absence of paradiplomatic action, but, since it is developed within a legal void, it depends mostly on political will. Secondly, sub-national governments receive no orientations in terms of administrative structure for international action. Consequently, these vary widely from one state to another and even from one political mandate to another. Thirdly, different legal frameworks are created from one state to another and from one city to another within their state constitutions and municipal laws (BRANCO, 2007). Finally, a posture which has been frequently adopted – with success – to circumvent subnational governments' incapacity to sign international treaties and agreements has been for them to take on a role of mediation in international activities between private entities or to take part in international sub-national networks as well as in decentralised cooperation programmes (PRADO, 2011).

However, the Federal State accepts with difficulty the involvement of new actors in foreign policy, fearing a weakening of national policies. Most cases of paradiplomatic actions involve some participation from the Ministry of Foreign Affairs' Federative Relations Advisory Board[84] (VIGEVANI, 2006), demonstrating limited capacity of action by political entrepreneurs. Additionally, financial resources are concentrated within the Federal State, making it difficult for sub-national governments to increase their remit and actions (BRANCO, 2007).

In practice, Brazilian paradiplomatic activity mostly focuses, as in many countries, on areas belonging to *low politics* such as education, culture or tourism, with the deliberate intention not to create conflicts with State foreign policy (VIGEVANI, 2006).

Researchers (CHAUI, 2006; RUBIM, 2011; OLIVEIRA, 2012) tend to date back the emergence of cultural policies in Brazil to the 1930s, carried amongst others by Mário de Andrade from the cultural department of São Paulo city council and by intellectuals such as Gustavo Capanema at the beginning of Getúlio Vargas's government (1930–1945). However, cooperation between different levels of government in terms of cultural policies was only established officially in 2012 with the creation of the National Cultural System[85] which required a modification of the Brazilian constitution.[86]

This system, "organised in a collaborative manner, in a decentralised and participatory way, establishes a process of joint management and promotion of cultural public policies" (Brasil, Constituição, 1988,[87] art. 216-A, § 1). It included, amongst others, the following principles: "IV– cooperation between federal bodies, public and private agents involved in the cultural sector"; "V – integration and interaction in the carrying out of policies, programmes, projects and actions"; "VIII – autonomy of federal bodies and of civil society institutions"; "XI – coordinated and agreed decentralisation of management, resources and actions"; and "XII – progressive increase of the public budgets dedicated to culture" (Brasil, Constituição, 1988, art. 216-A, §1).

It also more generally affirmed the importance of the creation of public policies for culture and the autonomy and collaboration of different levels of government for their implementation: "The States, the Federal District and the Municipalities will organise their own cultural systems in dedicated laws" (Brasil, Constituição, 1988, art. 216-A, §4). Following the enactment of this law and with the help of the Ministry of Culture, a number of Brazilian states including Rio Grande do Sul developed state Cultural Plans[88] (CALABRE, 2013).

A study (MARIÉ, 2018) attempted to identify the evolution of the cultural components of Rio Grande do Sul state's paradiplomacy from 1987 (year of the creation of the first paradiplomatic apparatus in Rio Grande do Sul) to 2014 through an analysis of the evolution of the place given to culture in the state's paradiplomatic institutions and agenda throughout the period.

Through a sequence analysis, three phases were identified in terms of space given to culture within the paradiplomatic institutional framework: a phase of expansion (1987–1994), followed by a phase of retraction (1995–2010), followed by another phase of expansion (2011–2015). In the first phase, RS' paradiplomacy was carried out by the SEAI (Special Secretariat for International Affairs[89]), which gave significant institutional space to cultural questions. Furthermore, the institutionalisation of the cultural sector in RS came jointly with a discourse around the use of culture for integration with La Plata basin neighbours. In the second phase, the paradiplomatic structure was modified to focus more and more on economic issues, setting aside low-priority sectors such as culture. Institutional innovation in the third phase, through a new horizontal framework, made space for international action in all sectors of the State's activity, including cultural issues (MARIÉ, 2018).

In terms of space given to cultural issues in the paradiplomatic agenda, phases are divided slightly differently from those identified in the evolution of the institutional framework: a phase of will tampered by a lack of means (1987–1990), followed by a phase of focus on questions other than culture (1991–2010), followed by a phase of construction of an incipient cultural paradiplomatic agenda and discourse (2011–2015). During the first one, an ambitious agenda included some cultural aspects, mostly focused on Latin America, but results were tampered by a lack of budget and staffing. The second phase is characterised by a focus on economic relations, and thus, culture was virtually absent from RS's paradiplomacy during this period. In the third phase, the paradiplomatic agenda was diversified, thus bringing cultural aspects back in (MARIÉ, 2018).

Furthermore, although a discursive element around the gaúcha identity is definitely present in RS at least since the 1980s (PINTO, 2011), this identity can be seen mostly within the State and projected in the rest of the country. The projection of this identity beyond national borders is not very strong, due at least partly to a lack of institutional structure. A discursive element around the international cultural projection of the RS State was identified exclusively in the third phase. It can be seen as linked to the will to project a stronger

72 *Cultural governance in the Brazil-Uruguay borderlands*

image of RS which was present in this phase, but also to factors of a cultural nature at national and local level. In 2012, the establishment of a national framework for culture pushed many states, amongst which RS, to establish their own cultural frameworks and to perceive the importance of culture as a public policy. In this sense, we see that the development path of cultural policies had an influence on that of cultural paradiplomacy.

Tables 4.3 and 4.4 are drawn from the analysis of the evolution of the state's paradiplomacy and cultural policies throughout the period. In the first one, which shows the evolution of the state's paradiplomatic and cultural institutional framework, the institutional bodies which could lead cultural actions in the borderlands are highlighted. In the second one, which shows the evolution of RS's international relations agenda, the topics related to borderlands and cultural policy are highlighted.

Table 4.3 Evolution of RS's paradiplomatic and cultural institutional frameworks

Mandate	Governor	Party	Institutional structure/international relations	Institutional structure/culture
1987–1991	Pedro Simon	PMDB (Brazilian Democratic Movement)	SEAI (Special Secretariat for International Affairs[90]) (1) International cooperation (2) Private investments **(3) Latin American integration** ***Integration; Cultural Cooperation***	CODEC (Cultural Development Council[91]) - **Integration of the La Plata basin countries** - **Promotion of the gaúcha identity** - International cultural exchange
1991–1995	Alceu de Deus Collares	PDT (Democratic Labour Party)	SEAI (1) International Cooperation Department *Technical International Cooperation; Technical Cooperation with Developing Countries; Technical Cooperation with Partner-States* (2) Business Department *International Events; Business Cooperation and Promotion* (3) Latin American Integration Department *Information & Documentation;* ***Border Issues; Cultural Integration;*** *Latin American Studies*	

Cultural governance in the Brazil-Uruguay borderlands 73

Table 4.3 Continued

Mandate	Governor	Party	Institutional structure/ international relations	Institutional structure/culture
1995–1999	Antônio Britto	PMDB	[1995–1996] SEDAI (Development and International Affairs Secretariat[92]) (1) Latin American integration (2) International cooperation and business [1996–1999] SEDAI Department for International Affairs and Latin American Integration *Latin American Integration; International Cooperation; International Business; International Business Networks; Consular Relations*	**State Lei de Incentivo à Cultura**[93] **(1996)**
1999–2003	Olívio Dutra	PT (Workers' Party)	SEDAI Department for International Affairs and Latin American Integration (1) International Business (2) International Affairs # Special Office for Mercosul Affairs[94]	

2003–2007	Germano Rigotto	PMDB	SEDAI
			Department for International Affairs and Latin American Integration
			(1) International Business
			  International Fairs Sector; Exporter Room
			(2) International Affairs
			  International Cooperation; Consular Relations; International Governmental Missions; Latin American Affairs	

2007–2011	Yeda Crusius	PSDB (Brazilian Social Democracy Party)	SEDAI (1) Department for International Affairs (2) Department for Business Development (3) Department for the Promotion of Investments (4) Sales Board	
2011–2015	Tarso Genro	PT	**ACRI (Advisory Board for Cooperation and International Relations**[95]**)**	**State Cultural Plan (2012)**

Credit: Solène Marié

74 Cultural governance in the Brazil-Uruguay borderlands

Table 4.4 Evolution of RS's paradiplomatic agenda

Mandate	Governor	Party	IR priorities	Main partners
1987–1991	Pedro Simon	PMDB (Brazilian Democratic Movement)	Regional integration **Border and infrastructure development** Cultural and academic exchange	South Cone countries The USA Spain Japan
1991–1995	Alceu de Deus Collares	PDT (Democratic Labour Party)	Economic relations	South Cone countries
1995–1999	Antônio Britto	PMDB	Economic relations	South Cone countries Japan Canada The USA
1999–2003	Olívio Dutra	PT (Workers' Party)	Economic relations Technical cooperation	South Cone countries Canada European countries
2003–2007	Germano Rigotto	PMDB	Economic relations	South Cone countries Other partners: ad hoc
2007–2011	Yeda Crusius	PSDB (Democratic Labour Party)	Economic relations	South Cone countries Italy Other partners: ad hoc
2011–2015	Tarso Genro	PT	Economic relations (agriculture) Political-institutional relations **Cultural relations Relations with Latin American countries**	South Cone countries Cuba Manitoba (Canada) Shiga (Japan) Chungcheongnam-do (South Korea)

Cedit: Adapted from MARIÉ, 2018

The analysis of the evolution of RS's international relations agenda generally highlights the following characteristics: short-term planning and *ad hoc* projects (NUNES, 2005), corresponding more to government development policies than to a proper State development policy (FERREIRA, 2015).

The repeated changes throughout the period show that the RS state government has not settled on a long-term formula (SALOMÓN & NUNES, 2007). Furthermore, they also demonstrate the strong influence which the interests, vision and actions of each governor have on RS's paradiplomacy. Therefore, the development of long-term cultural public policy at state level is rendered difficult and makes state initiation of or support to cultural actions difficult, be it in the borderlands or in general.

Putting these observations in perspective with the challenges generally faced by sub-national governments in the South in their international cultural action as highlighted by cultural policy literature, the following comments can be made.

Firstly, institutional structure plays a crucial role in enabling cultural paradiplomacy and in fostering cultural production which is distinct from that which is projected by the central government (ZAMORANO; MORATÓ, 2014). A study of the internationalisation and paradiplomacy of creative cities conducted in Brazil highlighted five factors which contribute to the development of an assertive paradiplomacy by the latter: segmentation of the city, qualified sub-national bureaucracies, harmonious relations between central and municipal governments, autonomy conceded to municipalities and interdependence of the city (JESUS, 2017). In line with this criteria, the study of RS's cultural paradiplomacy demonstrates a lack of autonomy and of qualified bureaucracy at state level which hinders the state's ability to support the development of cultural production in the borderlands.

Secondly, cultural policies are a particularly complex area of public policy because of their profoundly cross-sectional nature. In terms of policy areas, they often cross over into sectors such as tourism, education or foreign policy, amongst others. Also, they involve public policies at various levels of government as well as the private and third sectors. Furthermore, they are intrinsically long-term policies. The resulting complexities in terms of governance are felt particularly strongly in low-income countries with incipient institutions, where public policies suffer from discontinuity and where there is a lack of professionals with specialised training (ISAR, 2008).

The cross-sectional nature of cultural policy also implies that cultural projects are incorporated within larger projects from other areas, for example in education (REIS, 2008). The consequence of this is that projects are geared towards culture and development – the contribution of culture to development – rather than cultural development – the development of cultures and cultural capacities (EPSKAMP; GOULD, 2000). In practice, many Brazilian regions struggle to operationalise cultural development policies, due to a lack of articulation between regional and cultural policies along with a lack of actions which aim to value local culture (SANTOS, 2015).

These difficulties in terms of development of local cultural policies are naturally felt even more in terms of internationalisation of these policies. Yet, the valuing and protection of a local culture at sub-national level is an essential first step in its later internationalisation: "there is a clear connection between the foreign action and the adoption of local cultural policies" (ZAMORANO; MORATO, 2014, p. 11)

4.1.4 Contribution of the municipalities to cultural governance in the borderlands

Despite the existence in the borderlands of some federal actions of varying degrees of effectiveness, as presented previously, the Brazilian government itself is aware of the weakness of these programmes. In the 2009 document produced to present the PDFF,[96] the then Secretary of Regional Programmes[97] wrote the following about the Brazilian Border Strip:

> Despite its strategic nature for South American integration [...] the Border Strip constitutes an economically underdeveloped region, historically abandoned by the State, marked by the difficulty of access to public goods and services, by a lack of social cohesion, by disregard for citizenship and by problems which are specific to border regions.
>
> (BRASIL, 2009, p. 8)

In borderlands, flows and their institutionalisation can be categorised based on their nature and origin. Osório Machado (1998, p. 4) makes a distinction, in terms of networks, between the "spontaneous order" and the "organised order". According to her, the understanding of these networks "is fundamental to the understanding of the State's and populations' changes of perspective in relation to boundaries and borders" (OSÓRIO MACHADO, 1998, p. 4). Similarly, we can divide integration initiatives between those which would in generic terms correspond to a bottom-up or a top-down process, mostly referred to in Brazilian literature on the subject as local and summit integration. Local integration would correspond to the immediate, social integration of borderlanders' daily lives. The second is the result of actions from individuals located at the institutional top levels of states, through instruments such as events, agreements and laws (BENTO, 2015a).

Whilst it does not need the institutionalisation of the State's core in order to exist, local integration in the borderlands (the spontaneous order) is qualified by the recognition and institutionalisation operated by the summit (the organised order). These benefits are particularly felt in areas such as health, social services and education, in which the creation of specific legal frameworks for borderlands makes it easier for them to overcome the inadequacy of laws created in the centres of power in relation to their own reality (BENTO, 2015a).

Local integration largely preceded summit integration in the Brazil-Uruguay borderlands. The former

> isn't an original production of the political-legal-administrative centres of the State, but an avant-garde creation, even if it is involuntary, of populations from integrated border cities.
>
> (BENTO, 2015a)

Based on the historical informal integration operated locally, the first efforts in the direction of structured integration and cooperation in the borderlands started in 1989 with the creation of the Border Committees of twin cities.[98] These committees are composed of members of municipal administration and occasionally invite members of the civil society involved in social, economic and cultural activities in the borderlands (LEMOS; RÜCKERT, 2011).

Two decades later, on the 21st of March 2014, twin cities were officially recognised and defined by the Ministry of National Integration.[99] An interesting fact is that this officialisation was made, amongst other justifications brought forward in the preamble of the provision, "in view of the increasing demands by the municipalities for specific public policies for these cities" and "considering the importance of twin cities for border integration and, consequently, for South American integration". Clearly, the institutionalisation process identified here is of a bottom-up nature, stemming from demands from local actors. Also, the action from the federal government which followed local action was conceived as contributing to the wider objective of regional integration. Three levels of government can be identified here: a local catalyst, a national institutionalisation and a regional objective.

The provision thus defines border twin cities through two criteria:

1 "Their location: municipalities cut by the border line, be it dry or on a waterway, articulated or not by infrastructure work, which present great potential for economic and cultural integration, with or without a conurbation or semi-conurbation with a locality in the neighbouring country, as well as "condensed" manifestations of problems which are typical of borders, which acquire greater density there, with direct effects on regional development and citizenship".
2 Their population: only municipalities composed of at least 2,000 inhabitants individually can be considered part of a twin city.

In 2002, horizontal integration in the borderlands led to another important vertical institutionalisation of this integration, or, in other words, claims from the periphery led to action at the core. Following a movement led by civil society (the Border Committees of twin cities) demanding public policies that suited the reality of the border, the previously mentioned New Agenda for Cooperation and Border Development between Brazil and Uruguay was elaborated. It constituted a response from the centre of the states involved to the observation of flaws in the articulation of the different levels of institutional presence in the borderlands as well as weaknesses in actions previously led by the Border Committees. In this way, it represented "an adaptation of the two states to the reality of local integration at the Brazilian-Uruguayan border" (LEMOS; RÜCKERT, 2014, p. 153).

Also, this initiative represented a new impulse for the Border Committees of twin cities, which had progressively lost momentum throughout the 1990s and were reducing the frequency of their meetings due to reduced capacity to reach significant results (AVEIRO, 2006). The signature of the bilateral agreement provided renewed impetus to the committees which were revived through their new role as an intermediate channel between local communities and federal institutions (LEMOS; RÜCKERT, 2011).

Furthermore, the creation of the Borderland Integration Zone as part of the New Agenda tackled the long-running problem of the "undocumented"[100]: Uruguayans or Brazilians who lived, studied or worked on the other side of the border without legal authorisation to do so, through the creation of the "Special Borderlander ID".[102] However, in 2009, the number of applicants decreased due to the coming into force of Mercosul's Agreement on the Residence of Nationals of Mercosul Member States and from Bolivia and Chile,[101] negotiated in 2002. As the latter applies to spaces outside of the borderlands and gives access to permanent citizenship after two years, borderlanders thereafter preferred it to the Special Borderlander ID and the number of requests dropped. In Rivera, the number of applicants went from 108 in 2004 to 14 in 2010 (LEMOS; RÜCKERT, 2011).

Therefore, although local integration precedes summit integration in this case, we can say that the latter reinforces and facilitates the process by reducing legal barriers and creating programmes that enable an intensification of already existing interactions between populations. The case of the decrease in applications for Special Borderlander Documents linked to the creation of new policies by the Mercosul provides the counterpoint for arguing that whilst the force of local policies is that they are specific, the force of summit integration, when it is effective, is that it is far-reaching.

A common feature of all the different versions of the PDFF is to view local actors and especially Border Committees of twin cities as central to initiatives in the borderlands (BRASIL, 2005, 2009, 2017). As formulated in the 2009 Cartilha da Faixa de Fronteira:

> Despite the low degree of institutionalisation usually observed in Border Committees, there is evidence of their effectiveness on the border between Brazil and Uruguay.
>
> (BRASIL, 2009, p. 22)

The latter are seen as the local executive bodies of the action plans, thereafter reporting to the consulates (BRASIL, 2009).

On the other hand, the Ministry of National Integration also recognises the historical difficulty linked to political and institutional structures which do not reflect the needs of local populations. This engenders difficulties for them in passing on their demands to higher levels of government (DA SILVA; CALDEIRÃO, 2018). In 2009, for example, 90% of the PDFF's budget derived from a type of funds allocated to Congresspeople for the fulfilment of engagements made during their campaigns,[103] which are usually spent in their electoral strongholds. With the exception of a few larger municipalities situated in the Border Strip, it is a big challenge for small borderland municipalities to apply for and take part in this type of federal programmes for reasons linked to institutional weaknesses (CARNEIRO; CAMARA, 2019).

This is evidenced through Da Silva and Caldeirão's (2018) previously mentioned study which reports that, when asked to make spontaneous suggestions of factors which would support the development of the border strip, Jaguarão municipal employees mentioned (1) the importance of training for municipal civil servants, (2) the creation of binational agreements for Jaguarão-Río Branco and (3) further information and clarifications on the topic of heritage (included in PDFF programmes). Whilst they are in a front-line position in terms of execution of programmes and passing on of demands to higher spheres of government, municipal employees lack both awareness of programmes in which they are taking part and information on how to access other existing programmes. This can be related to the "institutional distance between these regions and the state" (MERCHER; BERNARDO; SILVA, 2018), which superimposes itself upon the physical distance.

Mercher, Bernardo and Silva's (2018) study of South American cities' actions towards integration in the borderlands through the Mercocities network sees the institutional gap which results from lack of action from central governments as a window of opportunity for sub-national units to get involved in the issue. Amongst the various existing city networks, the one which is most closely connected to the needs and agenda of smaller, peripheral municipalities throughout South America is the Mercocities Network.[104] In spite of its name, the Mercocities Network is not a programme which stems from the Mercosul itself: it was born out of municipal initiative and desire to cooperate.[105]

According to the authors, municipalities located in border conurbations have a significant presence within Mercocities, whilst it is not the case in other city networks. Furthermore, based on the initiative of border cities from the network, amongst others, a Border Integration Workgroup (UTIF[106]) was created in 2013. Border cities which took part in the creation of the working group were the following: Uruguaiana, Itaqui and Santa Vitória do Palmar (Brazil) and Asunción (Paraguay). Universities[107] are also recognised for having played a decisive role in the creation of the working group (MERCHER; BERNARDO; SILVA, 2018)

In general, of the total of 340 municipalities which take part in the network, 18 are situated in border conurbations[108]: Santa Vitória do Palmar, Paranhos, Coronel Sapucaia, Bela Vista, Barra do Quaraí, Guaíra and Foz do Iguaçu (Brazil); Rivera, Paysandú and Salto (Uruguay); Concordia and Posadas (Argentina); Assunção, Ypehú, Bella Vista Norte, Salto del Guairá, Pedro Juan Caballero (Paraguay); and Arica (Chile) (MERCHER; BERNARDO; SILVA, 2018, pp. 15–16).

They offer the following inventory of actions led by member cities through the network as well as independently, divided in seven categories: social, development, tourism, culture, environment, urbanism and security. In Table 4.5, initiatives in the border conurbation of Santana do Livramento-Rivera are underlined.

The analysis of this table shows that whilst numerous actions were led in those cities, those in the cultural sector are a minority: out of the 36 initiatives, only 1 relates to culture. Two initiatives can be found in the border

Cultural governance in the Brazil-Uruguay borderlands

Table 4.5 Initiatives from Mercocities's conurbated border city members

Category	Initiatives
Social	1 Coronel Sapucaia: Environmental Education of Brazil-Paraguay Border Region [Brazil/Paraguay] 2 Coronel Sapucaia: Intercultural Border Schools Programme [Brazil] 3 Paysandú: Binational Agricultural School of Paysandú/Guaviyu Technical School [Uruguay/Argentina] 4 Paysandu, Rivera: Joint policies for vulnerable young people [Uruguay/Argentina] 5 Clorinda, Encarnacion, Posadas: Agreement on migration policies [Argentina/Paraguay] 6 Arica, Tacna: Covenant on academic integration through Tarapaca University [Peru/Chile] 7 Pedro Juan Caballero, Ponta Porã: Binational Parliament [Paraguay/Brazil] 8 Bella Vista Norte, Bela Vista: Binational Parliament [Paraguay/Brazil] 9 Pedro Juan Caballero, Ponta Porã: Intercultural Bilingual Border School [Paraguay/Brazil]
Development	1 Coronel Sapucaia: Promote Borders Project [Brazil] 2 Foz do Iguaçu: Brazil - Argentina Border Committee [Brazil/Argentina] 3 Foz do Iguaçu: Movement for the Border Identification Card [Argentina/Brazil/Paraguay] 4 Concordia, Salto: Common agenda for international cooperation [Argentina/Uruguay] 5 Barra do Quaraí: Bilateral programme for technical assistance in governability [Brazil] 6 Foz do Iguaçu: Hosting of the International Seminar on Border Regions [Brazil] 7 Posadas, Garupa, Candelaria, Encarnación: Creation of a binational urban conglomerate [Argentina/Paraguay] 8 Posadas-Encarnación: Integration Committee [Argentina/Paraguay] 9 Asunción, Clorinda: Optimisation Project for the Clorinda-Asunción urban node [Paraguay/Argentina] 10 Arica, Tacna: Integration of electrical power grids [Chile/Peru] 11 Pedro Juan Caballero, Ponta Porã: Revitalisation of the international border line [Paraguay/Brazil] 12 Pedro Juan Caballero, Ponta Porã: Creation of a popular market [Paraguay/Brazil]
Tourism	1 Foz do Iguaçu: Meeting focusing on the discussion of problems of mobility/road transportation at the border with Paraguay [Brazil/Paraguay] 2 Foz do Iguaçu: Integrated Tourism Routes project [Brazil/Argentina/Uruguay] 3 Rivera, Paysandu: Members of the group of municipalities taking part in the TCHÊ Route [Argentina/Uruguay]
Culture	1 Arica: Hosting of a Latin American meeting of "cueca" folk dance [Chile]

(*Continued*)

Cultural governance in the Brazil-Uruguay borderlands 81

Table 4.5 (Continued)

Category	Initiatives
Environment	1 Foz do Iguaçu, Puerto Iguazu, Ciudad del Este: Joint sustainable development project [Brazil/Argentina/Paraguay] 2 Concordia, Salto: Environmental policies to protect the Guarani Aquifer [Argentina/Uruguay] 3 Rivera, Santana do Livramento: Environmental policies to protect the Guarani Aquifer [Uruguay/Brazil] 4 Ponta Porã, Pedro Juan Caballero: Environmental policies to protect the Guarani Aquifer [Paraguay/Brazil] 5 Pedro Juan Caballero e Ponta Porã: Integrated river management [Paraguay/Brazil]
Urbanism	1 Pedro Juan Caballero e Ponta Porã: Joint urban planning [Paraguay/Brazil] 2 Bella Vista Norte e Bela Vista: Joint urban planning [Paraguay/Brazil] 3 Posadas: Strategic urban planning, with the perspective of integration with border cities [Argentina] 4 Posadas: Urban Integration and Environmental Quality: Mobility, transport and territorial articulation programme [Argentina] 5 Santana do Livramento e Rivera: Integrated urban planning providing border integration [Brazil/Uruguay]
Security	1 Foz do Iguaçu: Seminar on the prevention of cross-border crime [Brazil]

Credit: Reproduced and adapted from MERCHER; BERNARDO; SILVA, 2018

conurbation of Santana do Livramento-Rivera, but they are focused on urban and environmental issues.

Within the scope of the PDFF, a particularly successful initiative was set up in the educational sector: the Border Schools project,[109] which created binational courses and diplomas through a collaboration between the Consejo de Educación Técnico Profesional-Universidad del Trabajo del Uruguay (CETP-UTU) and the Instituto Federal Sul-Riograndense (IFSul).[110] This initiative stemmed from a 2006 project led by the Brazilian Cooperation Agency (ABC) and the United Nations Development Programme (UNDP) focused on regional development and capacity-building through which, in partnership with the two educational institutions, a series of short courses were offered to borderlanders (OTTE; ARAUJO; PACHALSKI, 2018). Thereafter, the creation of the Border Schools Project was a response from IFSul and CETP-UTU to a request from the Brazilian Ministry of Education within the framework of the PDFF, therefore jointly with the Ministry of National Integration with the participation of the local PDFF committees. A joint course was thus set up at IFSul in Santana do Livramento in 2010 and in Jaguarão in 2014 (*IFSUL; CETP-UTU, 2016*). Here, we can see a successful project in the borderlands which came to life based on the cooperation between a large number of organisations: an international institution (UNDP), a cooperation agency (ABC, led by the Brazilian Ministry of Foreign Affairs), a federal multi-level programme (PDFF) led by the Ministry of National Integration with local committees at municipal level, a ministry (MEC) and two educational institutions (CETP-UTU and IFSul). Literature and reports on the subject as well as interviews with professors involved in the process[111] point to the protagonism of the MEC, the ABC and the local educational institutions in contributing towards the success of the project: thus, institutions which specialise in the relevant sector (education) and in cooperation.

Notes

1 "Spaces near international borders in which the borderline, border policies or the relational processes inherent to border spaces, affect the everyday life of its inhabitants. As these processes vary from one borderland to another as well as within different areas of a specific borderland, the space which it includes on either side of the borderline cannot be defined with a fixed figure. Rather, borderlands take varying forms based on the relationships and networks which can be found across the borderline and their reach throughout space."
2 Which originates from the phrase *uti possidetis, ita possideatis* used by Roman judges in cases of private ownership.
3 José Maria da Silva Paranhos Jr, the "Barão do Rio Branco", Brazilian diplomat, politician and professor, largely responsible for the resolution of Brazil's border disputes and definition of these borders in their current form, through his actions as Minister of Foreign Affairs from 1902 to 1912.
4 *Províncias Unidas del Río de la Plata.*
5 Territory currently situated in the borderlands between Brazil and Argentina, displaying Jesuit Mission settlements which were built in the 17th and 18th centuries on lands which had previously been occupied by Guarani indigenous communities. Beyond the fact that their establishment stemmed from evangelisation campaigns, they also served the aim of systematic territorial occupation of the area.
6 *Banda Oriental del Uruguay.*
7 *Provincia Cisplatina.*
8 *República Oriental del Uruguay.*
9 *Tratado de Limites Tratado de Límites*
10 As defined by Palermo (2001): transition zone composed of the northern region of Uruguay, which constitutes a border region between Rio Grande do Sul, Brazil, and the coastal provinces of Argentina, mainly Entre Ríos.
11 Data from 2009.
12 Data from the 2011 census, most recent data available. Source: Instituto Nacional de Estadística (INE), Uruguay.
13 *Marco divisa Brasil/Uruguai*
14 *Ponte Internacional Barão de Mauá/Puente Internacional Barón de Mauá.*
15 Data from 2014.
16 Data from INE, 2011.
17 Industry that produces salted meat.
18 *Ciclo das charqueadas.*
19 In both cases, black enslaved populations who were an essential part of the crime-perpetuating Brazilian socio-economic system at the time.

20 Nowadays referred to as being "doble-chapa".
21 Original term in Spanish: *el hombre de front*era.
22 As well as in other states such as Mato Grosso and Amazonas.
23 Interview with Eduardo Palermo, History Professor and Director of the Museo del Patrimonio Regional de Rivera. Conducted by the author in Rivera, 18/09/2018.
24 Linguistic phenomenon which is largely present in the Brazil-Uruguay borderlands, as discussed more in detail in the subsequent paragraph.
25 Both spellings are used in academic literature. Thereafter, the spelling "portuñol" will be used as it is more frequently used in English language literature.
26 *Dialectos Portugueses del Uruguay.*
27 Interview with Eduardo Palermo. Op. cit.
28 Author of, amongst others: *Uma Terra Só*. São Paulo: Editora Melhoramentos, 1984; *Linha Divisória*. São Paulo: Editora Melhoramentos, 1988.
29 Interview with Berenice Farina da Rosa and Marcelo Flores da Cunha Garcia conducted by the author. Santana do Livramento, 20/09/2018.
30 *Reunión Especializada de Cultura.*
31 *Reunión de Ministros de la Cultura.*
32 CONGRESSO NACIONAL, REPRESENTAÇÃO BRASILEIRA NO PARLAMENTO DO MERCOSUL. **Protocolo de integração cultural do Mercosul.** Fortaleza, 1996.
33 *Parlamento Cultural de Mercosur.*
34 *Sistema de Información Cultural del Mercosur.*
35 *Programa Mercosur Audiovisual.*
36 *Fondo Mercosur Cultural.*
37 The text is currently being assessed by the Finances and Tax commission and has been so since the 9th of August 2019.
38 *Fondo para la Convergencia Estructural del Mercosur.*
39 *Grupo Ad Hoc Sobre Integración Fronteriza.*
40 Through Law n° 12.095, 19th of November 2009.
41 Interview with Dionéia de Macedo, Arts Professor at IFSUL. Conducted by the author in Santana do Livramento, 09/07/2018.
42 *Instituto do Patrimônio Histórico e Artístico Nacional.*
43 Composed of Law 6634, of 2nd of May 1979, Decree 85.064 of 1980 and article 20, §2 of the federal constitution of 1988.
44 *Conselho de Defesa Nacional.*
45 *Faixa de Segurança Nacional.*
46 *Conselho Superior de Segurança Nacional.*
47 A municipality, in the Brazilian context, refers to the smallest autonomous unit with a legal status in the federation. Its headquarters are situated in a town or city within the municipality which receives the name of the municipality and its seat. In rural areas, municipalities can have very large extensions and cover wide areas outside of their headquarters.
48 CÂMARA DOS DEPUTADOS. **Projeto propõe faixa de fronteira com largura diferenciada para cada estado.** Agência Câmara de Notícias: 13/15/2019.
49 MP from the MDB (Movimento Democrático Brasileiro) - Mato Grosso.
50 Bill 1144/19, submitted on the 26th of February, 2019.
51 Prior to this decade, the legislative debate on the topic was very limited except for processes linked to the regulation of the border strip.
52 Whilst Congresspeople from the Midwest, North and Southeast regions are responsible for, respectively, 21%, 11% and 2% of the bills. Furthermore, 12% of the bills were presented by commissions.
53 *Nova Agenda para Cooperação e Desenvolvimento Fronteiriço entre Brasil e Uruguai.*

84 Cultural governance in the Brazil-Uruguay borderlands

54 *Zona de Integração Fronteiriça.*
55 *Acordo para Permissão de Residência, Estudo e Trabalho a Nacionais Fronteiriços Brasileiros e Uruguaios.*
56 *Programa de auxílio financeiro dos municípios da Faixa de Fronteira.*
57 *Programa Social da Faixa de Fronteira.*
58 *Programa de Desenvolvimento da Faixa de Fronteira.*
59 *Programa de Promoção do Desenvolvimento da Faixa de Fronteira.* The abbreviation remained unchanged.
60 *Proposta de reestruturação do Programa de Desenvolvimento da Faixa de Fronteira.* The abbreviation remained unchanged.
61 *Bases para uma Proposta de Desenvolvimento e Integração da Faixa de Fronteira.*
62 *Comissão Permanente para o Desenvolvimento e a Integração da Faixa de Fronteira.*
63 *Núcleos Estaduais de Fronteira.*
64 *Planos de desenvolvimento e Integração das Faixas de Fronteira.*
65 *Programa para o Desenvolvimento da Faixa de Fronteira.*
66 *Comissão Permanente para o Desenvolvimento e a Integração da Faixa de Fronteira* (CDIF).
67 This study is based on Tibério Marques Schorn da Silva's experience of more than 10 years as a civil servant in the municipality of Jaguarão as well as his work as a researcher.
68 *Fronteira da Metade Sul do Rio Grande do Sul.*
69 *Festival de Cinema da Fronteira.*
70 Six local employees from three different departments of municipal administration (Planning and Urbanism, Administration, and Culture and Tourism). Three were civil servants with experience ranging various administrations; three were contract workers currently in high-level positions as Secretaries.
71 *Política Nacional de Desenvolvimento Regional.*
72 Interview with Mangela Britos, president of Jaguarão Cultural Municipal Council. Conducted by the author in Santana do Livramento, 13/09/2019.
73 *Conselho Municipal de Cultura*, council composed of members of the local civil society.
74 Field notes from an interview conducted by the author.
75 *Ministério das Relações Exteriores.*
76 *Departamento Cultural.*
77 Events which were agreed upon under the Cardoso administration, based on a proposition from French authorities
78 *Comissariado da cultura brasileira no Exterior.*
79 *Diretoria de Relações Internacionais.*
80 *Programa de Aceleração do Crescimento "Cidades Históricas".*
81 *Instituto do Patrimônio Histórico e Artístico Nacional.*
82 João Luiz Silva Ferreira, better known as Juca Ferreira, was Minister of Culture between 2008 and 2010 during the Luiz Inácio Lula da Silva administration and between 2015 and 2016 during the Dilma Rousseff administration.
83 *Diálogo da Fronteira.*
84 *Assessoria de Relações Federativas do Ministério das Relações Exteriores.*
85 *Sistema Nacional de Cultura.*
86 With PEC 71/2012 which added article 216-A to the Federal Constitution.
87 BRASIL. Constituição da República Federativa do Brasil. Brasília: 5 de outubro de 1988.
88 *Planos Estaduais de Cultura.*
89 *Secretaria Especial de Assuntos Internacionais.*
90 *Secretaria Especial de Assuntos Internacionais.*

91 *Conselho de Desenvolvimento da Cultura.*
92 *Secretaria do Desenvolvimento e dos Assuntos Internacionais.*
93 Programme which funds cultural actions through tax credits.
94 *Closed down in 2000.*
95 *Assessoria de Cooperação e Relações Internacionais.*
96 Commonly referred to as "Cartilha da Faixa de Fronteira".
97 Márcia Regina Sartori Damo.
98 *Comitês de Fronteira de cidades gêmeas.*
99 Through the following provision: BRASIL. Ministério da Integração Nacional. Gabinete do Ministro. **Portaria n. 125, de 21 de Março de 2014.**
100 *Os indocumentados.*
101 Through Decree n. 6.975, of 7th of October, 2009.
102 *Documento Especial de Fronteiriço.*
103 Funds known as "emenda parlamentar".
104 Contrary, for example, to the South American Cities Network (REDCISUR) whose action revolves more around large cities, and to Red Andina de Ciudades (RAC) whose action is focused on a specific area: the Andes.
105 The idea of the network arised in 1995 during a meeting of the Union of Ibero-American Capital Cities (União de Cidades Capitais Ibero-Americanas, in Portuguese). The creation of the network was formalized later the same year through the signature of the founding act of Mercociudades in the city of Asunción in July 1995.
106 *Unidade Temática de Integração Fronteiriça.*
107 Centro Universitário Ritter dos Reis and Laureate International Universities network.
108 This study focuses exclusively on border cities which are part of a conurbation: a junction of cities which compose a continuous urban area. It therefore does not include twin cities which do not merge together for a variety of reasons (geographic, political, urban, etc.).
109 *Projeto Escolas de Fronteira.*
110 CETP and IF are Uruguayan and Brazilian education institutions which focus on technical education.
111 Field notes from interviews with:
 - Lia Joan Nelson Pachalski, English professor at IFSUL and previously IR advisor (Pelotas, 04/07/2018)
 - César Augusto Azevedo Nogueira, mechanical engineering professor at IFSUL and current IR advisor (Pelotas, 04/07/2018)
 - Miguel Angelo Pereira Dinis, professor at IFSUL; teaching, research and outreach director; previously coordinator for binational actions (Santana do Livramento, 09/07/2018)

References

AMILHAT SZARY, A. Frontières et intégration régionale en Amérique Latine: sur la piste du chaînon manquant. In: FLAESCH-MOUGIN, C.; LEBULLENGER, J. [eds]. **Regards croisés sur les intégrations régionales Europe/Amériques**. Editions Bruylant, collection Rencontres Européennes, 2010, pp. 307–341.

AROCENA, F. [ed.]. **Regionalización cultural del Uruguay**. Montevideo: Universidad de la República, 2011.

ASEFF, L.C. **Memórias Boêmias, histórias de uma cidade de fronteira**. Masters thesis in history. Florianópolis: Universidade Federal de Santa Catarina, 2006.

AVEIRO, Thaís Mere Marques. **Relações Brasil-Uruguai**: A Nova Agenda para a Cooperação e o Desenvolvimento Fronteiriço. Brasília: Editora UNB, 2006.

BARÃO, Giulia Ribeiro. **A diplomacia cultural na política externa do governo Lula.** **Department of economics.** Porto Alegre: Universidade Federal do Rio Grande do Sul, 2012.
BENTO, Fábio Régio. Cidades-gêmeas e conurbadas de fronteira: na vanguarda da integração regional. In: PRADO, Henrique Sartori de Almeida; Espósito Neto, Tomaz [org.]. **Fronteiras e relações internacionais.** Curitiba: Ithala, 2015a, pp. 101–114.
BENTO, Fábio Régio. O papel das cidades gêmeas de fronteira na integração regional sul-americana. **Revista Conjuntura Austral,** v. 6, n. 27–28, pp. 50–53, dez. 2014-mar, 2015b.
BIJOS, L.; ARRUDA, V. A diplomacia cultural como instrumento de política externa brasileira. **Revista Dialogos: a cultura como dispositivo de inclusão,** v. 13, n. 1, pp. 33–53, 2010.
BORJA, Janira Trípodi. **A retórica do Silêncio: a cultura no Mercosul.** Master's degree dissertation: Universidade de Brasília, Instituto de Relações Internacionais, 2011.
BRANCO, Álvaro Chagas Castelo. A paradiplomacia como forma de inserção internacional de unidades subnacionais. **Prisma,** v. 4, n, 1, pp. 48–67, 2007.
BRASIL. Ministério da Integração Nacional. Secretaria de Programas Regionais. **Programa de Desenvolvimento da Faixa de Fronteira.** Proposta de Reestruturação do Programa de Desenvolvimento da Faixa de Fronteira. Brasília, 2005, 418p.
BRASIL. Ministério da Cultura. **Programa Cultural para o Desenvolvimento do Brasil.** Brasília, 2006.
BRASIL. **Cartilha do Programa de Desenvolvimento da Faixa de Fronteira** (PDFF). Brasília, 2009.
BRASIL. Ministério da Cultura. **Política Internacional do Ministério da Cultura:** 2003–2010. Documento interno, Brasília, DF, 2010.
BRASIL. Conselho de Defesa Nacional. Secretaria-Executiva. **Seminário Faixa De Fronteira:** Novos Paradigmas. Anexo 2.1.1. Brasília, 2011.
BRASIL. Secretaria de Assuntos Estratégicos. **Políticas de fronteira como fator de integração.** Diagnóstico das ações brasileiras nos espaços de fronteira. Brasília, 2013.
BRASIL. Ministério da Integração Nacional. **Consolidação dos planos de desenvolvimento e integração das faixas de fronteira.** Brasília, 2017.
CALABRE, Lia. Planos de cultura e suas diversas dimensões territoriais. In **Planos Estaduais de Cultura: desafios políticos e metodológicos.** 9th ENECULT Congress, Salvador, 11–13 September 2013.
CARNEIRO, C.P.; CAMARA, L.B. Políticas públicas na faixa de fronteira do Brasil: PDFF, CDIF e as políticas de segurança e defesa. **Confins-Revue Franco-Brésilienne de Géographie-Revista Franco-Brasileira de Geografia,** n. 41, 2019.
CARNEIRO FILHO, C.P.; LEMOS, B. de O. Brasil e Mercosul: Iniciativas de cooperação fronteiriça. **ACTA Geográfica,** 2014, pp. 203–219.
CHAUI, M. **Cidadania Cultural:** o Direito à Cultura. 2ª reimpressão. São Paulo: Ed. Fundação Perseu Abramo, 2006.
CHIAPPINI, Ligia. Multiculturalismo e identidade nacional. In: MARTINS, Maria Helena [org]. **Fronteiras Culturais. Brasil – Uruguai – Argentina.** Cotia: Ateliê Editorial, 2002
CHIAPPINI Ligia. **Mercosul Cultural e fronteiras.** Porto Alegre: Celpcyro, 2011.
CLEMENTE, Isabel. La Región De Frontera Uruguay-Brasil y La Relación Binacional: Pasado y Perspectivas. **Revista Uruguaya de Ciencia Política,** v. 19, n. 1, pp. 165–184, 2010.

COMUNELLO, F.J. O ativismo cultural e a imaginação da fronteira Brasil-Uruguai. **Civitas, Porto Alegre**, v. 18, n. 2, pp. 303–318, 2018

DA SILVA, T.M.S.; CALDEIRÃO, A.C. **Programa de Desenvolvimento da Faixa de Fronteira e sua aplicação no turismo de Jaguarão.** Jaguarão: Universidade Federal do Pampa, 2018.

DE SOUZA, Antônio Marcus Alves. **Cultura no Mercosul: Uma política do discurso.** Brasília: Plano Editora. Co-edição: Fundação Astrojildo Pereira, 2004.

DORFMAN, A. **Contrabandistas na Fronteira Gaúcha : Escalas Geográficas e Representações Textuais.** Doctoral thesis in geography. Florianópolis: UFSC, 2009.

ELIZAINCÍN, A., BEHARES, L. BARRIOS, G. **Nós falemo brasilero.** Dialectos Portugueses del Uruguay. Montevideo: Amesur, 1987.

EPSKAMP, Kees; GOULD, Helen. Outlining the debate. **Culturelink Review**, Special Issue, 2000.

FERNANDES, C.C.C.; RIBEIRO, M.F.B. **Políticas culturais para cidades mais criativas no Mercosul**: uma análise da paradiplomacia e cooperação descentralizada na rede Mercocidades. VI Seminário Internacional de Políticas Culturais. Fundação Casa de Rui Barbosa, Rio de Janeiro, Brasil. 26–29 May 2015.

FERREIRA, Bruno Guedes. **Atores públicos subnacionais e policia externa Brasileira: a paradiplomacia no Rio Grande do Sul (2007–2014)**. Dissertation (Master's degree in Social Sciences) - Faculdade de Filosofia e Ciências Humanas, Pontifícia Universidade Católica do Rio Grande do Sul, Porto Alegre, 2015, 165p.

FERREIRA, Roberta Lima. Difusão cultural e projeção internacional: O Brasil na América Latina (1937–45). In: SUPPO Hugo Rogelio, LESSA Monica Leite [eds]. **'A quarta dimensão da relações internacionais: a dimensão cultural'**. Rio de Janeiro: Contra Capa, 2012, pp. 65–88.

FRANÇA, A.B.C. **Nação e identidade na fronteira Brasil-Uruguai: uma análise a partir da cultura.** Porto Alegre: Universidade Federal do Rio Grande do Sul, 2016.

FRIZZO, Gabriela Neves; RIBEIRO, Maria de Fátima Bento; DE ÁVILA, Cristiane Bartz. "Uma Terra Só: Cultura, Interculturalidade na Fronteira entre Jaguarão, no Brasil e Rio Branco, no Uruguai". **Conexões Culturais – Revista de Linguagens, Artes e Estudos em Cultura**, v. 1, n. 2, 2015, pp. 268–283.

FURTADO, R.D.S. **Descobrindo a Faixa de Fronteira: A trajetória das elites organizacionais do executivo federal.** As estratégias, as negociações e o embate da constituinte. Curitiba: Editora CRV, 2013, 392p.

GOES FILHO, Synesio Sampaio. **Navegantes, bandeirantes, diplomatas. Um ensaio sobre a formação das fronteiras do Brasil.** Rio de Janeiro: Biblioteca do Exército Editora; São Paulo: Martins Fontes, 2000.

GOES FILHO, Synesio Sampaio. **As fronteiras do Brasil.** Brasília: FUNAG, 2013.

GRIMSON, Alejandro (comp). **Fronteras, naciones e identidades: La Periferia como Centro.** Ciccus-La Crujía, Buenos Aires, 2000.

HEREDIA, Edmundo A. O Cone Sul e a América Latina. In: **História do Cone Sul**. Rio de Janeiro: Revan, Brasília: EdUnB, 1998.

ISAR, Yudhishthir Raj. *Visão global: das inquietações conceituais a uma agenda de pesquisas. In: REIS, Ana Carla Fonseca [org.]. Economia criativa como estratégia de desenvolvimento: uma visão dos países em desenvolvimento. São Paulo : Itaú Cultural, 2008. 267 p.*

IFSUL; CETP-UTU. **Revista binacional. Parceria que deu certo: Educação Técnica na Fronteira**. 2016.

JACOB, Raúl. **Cruzando la frontera**. Montevideo: Arpoador, 2004.
JESUS, Diego Santos Vieira de. A arte do encontro: a paradiplomacia e a internacionalização das cidades criativas. **Revista de Sociologia e Política**, v. 25, n. 61, pp. 51–76, 2017.
LEMOS, B.D.O.; RÜCKERT, A.A. A região transfronteiriça Sant'Ana do Livramento-Rivera : cenários contemporâneos de integração/cooperação. **Revista de Geopolítica**, v. 2, n. 2, pp. 49–64, 2011.
LEMOS, B.D.O.; RÜCKERT, A.A. A Nova Agenda para Cooperação e Desenvolvimento Fronteiriço entre Brasil e Uruguai: repercussões territoriais nas cidades-gêmeas de Sant'Ana do Livramento e Rivera!. **Revista Política e Planejamento Regional (PPR)**, v. 1, n. 1, pp. 138–158, 2014.
LOSADA, Paula Ravanelli; SADECK, Bruno. O papel da fronteira na integração regional – o caso do consórcio intermunicipal da fronteira. In: PRADO, Henrique Sartori de Almeida; Espósito Neto, Tomaz [org.]. **Fronteiras e relações internacionais**. Curitiba: Ithala, 2015.
MARIÉ, Solène. Fronteiras brasileiras: evolução da agenda e redes de atores no Congresso Nacional (1990–2016). **Monções: Revista de Relações Internacionais da UFGD**, v. 6, pp. 50–78, 2017a.
MARIÉ, Solène. As políticas de diplomacia cultural nas gestões Cardoso e Lula em perspectiva comparada. In: **Dossiê cultura em foco: Integração cultural latinoamericana**. 1st ed. Jaguarão: Editora CLAEC, pp. 85–106, 2017b.
MARIÉ, Solène. **Cultural paradiplomacy institutions and agenda**: the case of Rio Grande do Sul, Brazil. Civitas: Revista de Ciências sociais, v. 18, n. 2, pp. 351–375, 2018.
MARTINS, Estevão Chaves de Rezende. **Cultura e Poder**. 2nd ed. São Paulo: Saraiva, 2007.
MASINA, Léa. A gauchesca brasileira: revisão crítica do regionalismo. In: MARTINS, Maria Helena [org]. **Fronteiras Culturais. Brasil – Uruguai – Argentina**. Cotia: Ateliê Editorial, 2002.
MERCHER, L.; BERNARDO, G.; SILVA, E. **South American Cities and Frontiers : an analysis of regional integration from Mercocities Network**. Working paper presented at the International Studies Association annual convention, San Francisco, April 2018.
MILANI, Carlos R.S; RIBEIRO, M.C.M. International relations and the paradiplomacy of Brazilian cities: crafting the concept of local international management. **BAR**, v. 8, n. 1, pp. 21–36, 2011.
MINEIRO, Procópio. Mercosul pensa cultura. In **Cadernos do terceiro mundo**, n. 225, 2000, pp. 22–27.
MOREIRA, Marcelo Ribeiro et al. A Integração Transfronteiriça na Faixa de Fronteira: Limites e Possibilidades para a Ação do Ministério da Integração Nacional. In **Boletim Regional**. Informativo da Política Nacional de Desenvolvimento Regional. n° 7 (maio/agosto). Brasília: Ministério da Integração Nacional. Secretaria de Políticas de Desenvolvimento Regional, 2008.
MÜLLER, Karla Maria. Práticas comunicacionais em espaços de fronteira: os casos do Brasil-Argentina e Brasil-Uruguai. In: MARTINS, Maria Helena [org]. **Fronteiras Culturais. Brasil – Uruguai – Argentina**. Cotia: Ateliê Editorial, 2002.
NUNES, Carmen Juçara da Silva. **A paradiplomacia no Brasil: O caso do Rio Grande do Sul**, 2005. 163p. Dissertation (Master's degree in International

Relations) – Programa de Pós-graduação em Relações Internacionais, Universidade Federal do Rio Grande do Sul, Porto Alegre, 2005.

OLIVEIRA, Paulo Augusto Almeida de. **Novo Paradigma de Política Cultural Brasileira**. As Políticas Públicas, de governo e de Estado. VIII Encontro de Estudos Multidisciplinares em Cultura (ENECULT). Salvador, Bahia, Brazil. 8–10 August 2012.

OLIVEN, Ruben G. Algunas Claves Socioculturales para entender Rio Grande do Sul. **Cuadernos para el Debate n. 5**. Programa de Investigaciones Socioculturales en el Mercosur. Instituto de Desarrollo Económico y Social (IDES). Buenos Aires, 1999.

OSÓRIO MACHADO, Lia. Limites, fronteiras, redes. In: STROHAECKER, T. et al. [Ed.]. **Fronteiras e espaço global**. pp. 41–49, 1998.

OTTE, J.; ARAUJO, J.J.; PACHALSKI, L. Cooperação IFSul e CETP UTU na faixa de fronteira : o empoderamento discursivo de atores locais na construção de uma política internacional com relevante impacto social. **RELACult – Revista Latino-Americana de Estudos em Cultura e Sociedade**, v. 4, n. ed. especial, pp. 1–15, 2018.

PALERMO, Eduardo. **Banda Norte, una historia de la frontera oriental, de indios, contrabandistas, misioneros y esclavos**. Rivera: Yatay, 2001.

PALERMO, E. **Terra brasiliensis. La región histórica del Norte uruguayo en la segunda mitad del siglo XIX- 1850–1900**. Porto Alegre: FCM, 2019.

PANITZ, L.M. Pratiques musicales, représentations et transterritorialités en réseau entre l' Argentine, le Brésil et l' Uruguay. **Géographie et cultures**, n. 88, 2015.

PANITZ, L.M. **Redes musicais e [re]composições territoriais no Prata: por uma Geografia da Música em contextos multi-localizados**. Doctoral thesis in geography. Porto Alegre: UFRGS, 2016.

PINTO, Muriel. **A construção da identidade missionária no Rio Grande do Sul e as políticas culturais no sul do Brasil**. Dissertation (Master's degree in Regional Development) - Programa de Pós-Graduação em Desenvolvimento Regional, Universidade de Santa Cruz do Sul – UNISC, Santa Cruz do Sul, 2011, 154p.

PRADO, Henrique Sartori de Almeida. **A paradiplomacia no processo de integração regional: o caso do Mercosul**. 3rd ABRI National Congress, São Paulo, 20–22 July 2011. Proceedings online.

REIS, Ana Carla Fonseca [org.]. **Economia criativa como estratégia de desenvolvimento: uma visão dos países em desenvolvimento**. São Paulo: Itaú Cultural, 2008, 267p.

ROCCA, Pablo. Encruzilhadas e fronteiras da gauchesca (Do Rio da Prata ao Rio Grande do Sul). In: MARTINS, Maria Helena [org]. **Fronteiras Culturais. Brasil – Uruguai – Argentina**. Cotia: Ateliê Editorial, 2002.

RUBIM, Antônio Albino Canelas. **As Políticas Culturais e o Governo Lula**. São Paulo: Ed. Fundação Perseu Abramo, 2011.

SALOMÓN, Mónica; NUNES, Carmen. A Ação Externa dos Governos Subnacionais no Brasil. Os Casos do Rio Grande do Sul e de Porto Alegre. Um Estudo Comparativo de Dois Tipos de Atores Mistos. **Contexto Internacional**, Rio de Janeiro, v. 29, n. 1, janeiro/junho 2007, pp. 99–147.

SANTOS, Valcir Bispo. **A relação entre cultura e desenvolvimento e a estratégia de fomento de arranjos criativos na Amazônia**. VI Seminário Internacional de Políticas Culturais. Fundação Casa de Rui Barbosa, Rio de Janeiro, Brasil. 26–29 May 2015.

SCHERMA, Márcio Augusto. As fronteiras nas relações internacionais. In: PRADO, Henrique Sartori de Almeida; Espósito Neto, Tomaz [org.]. **Fronteiras e relações internacionais**. Curitiba: Ithala, 2015.

SIMI, G. **Between the Line: The Semiotics of Everyday Life in the Brazil-Uruguay Borderlands**. Doctoral thesis in cultural studies. Nottingham: University of Nottingham, 2018.

SOARES, Maria Susana Arrosa. **A diplomacia cultural no Mercosul**. Brasília: Revista Brasileira de Política Internacional, v. 51, n. 1, pp. 53–69, 2008.

STURZA, E. Portunhol: língua , história e política. **Gragoatá**, v. 24, n. 48, pp. 95–116, 2019.

VIGEVANI, Tullo. Problemas para a atividade internacional das unidades subnacionais. Estados e municípios brasileiros. **Revista Brasileira de Ciências Sociais**, v. 21, n. 62, pp. 127–169, 2006.

ZAMORANO, Mariano Martín; MORATÓ, Arturo Rodríguez. The cultural paradiplomacy of Barcelona since the 1980s: understanding transformations in local cultural paradiplomacy. **International Journal of Cultural Policy**, v. 21, n. 5. pp. 554–576, 2014.

5 Cultural governance in the France-Germany borderlands

Formal and informal dynamics

5.1 Geographical contextualisation

The border which France shares with Germany reaches a total of 451 km, making it the fifth longest (after the borders with Spain, Switzerland, Belgium and Italy) of the total of eight borders which France shares with other countries. In terms of relative length, it represents 15.61% of the 2,889 km of land borders which metropolitan France shares with neighbours (including only continental France, excluding French overseas islands and territories).

This part of the border starts at the triple border between Luxembourg, France and Germany (coordinates 49°28′10″N, 6°22′2″E) at the encounter between the municipalities of Apach (in the French *département* of Moselle), Perl (in the German *Land* of Saarland) and Schengen (in the *kantonen* of Remich in Luxembourg), situated around the Moselle river. From this point, it follows east until the Rhine, whose course marks the borderline southwards until the triple border between Switzerland, France and Germany (coordinates 47°35′23″N, 7°35′21″E). This point is situated at the encounter between the municipalities of Huningue (in the French *département* of Haut-Rhin), Weil am Rhein (in the German *Land* of Baden-Württemberg) and Basel (in the Swiss *kanton* of Basel-Stadt) (Figure 5.1).

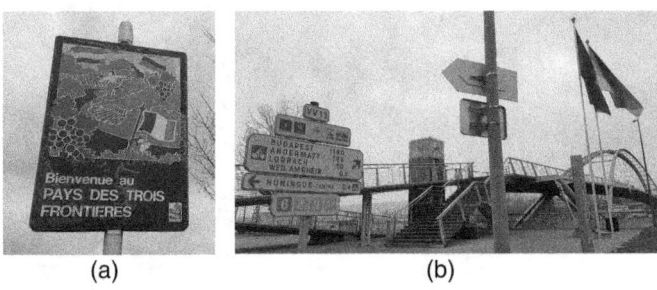

(a)   (b)

Figure 5.1 Images from the northern (a) and southern (b) edges of the France-Germany borderline

Credit: Solène Marié

DOI: 10.4324/9781003413400-5

92 *Cultural governance in the France-Germany borderlands*

Figures 5.2–5.4 indicate the localisation of these borderlands and situates them within the subcontinent and within the region. As in the case of the Brazil-Uruguay borderlands, the aim of these maps is not to delineate precisely the limits of the borderlands but to provide contextualisation and visualisation.

In terms of administrative units, this border region includes the German *Land* of Saarland, Rhineland-Palatinate and Baden-Württemberg, as well as the

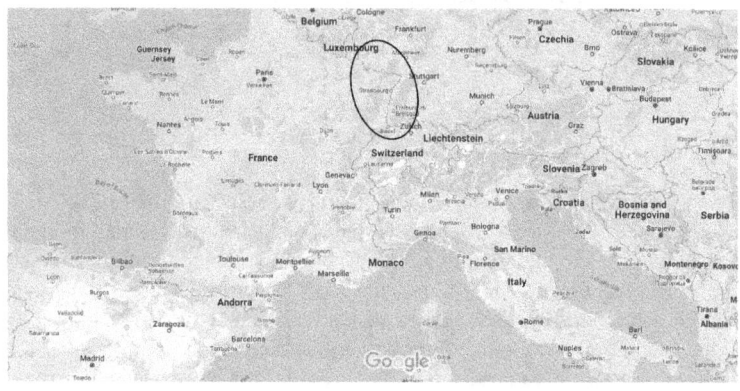

Figure 5.2 Location of the France-Germany borderlands within the sub-continent
Credit: Google

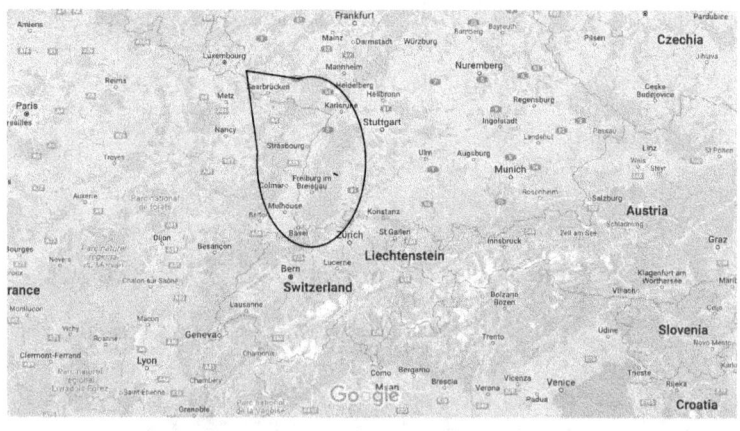

Figure 5.3 Location of the France-Germany borderlands within the region
Credit: Google

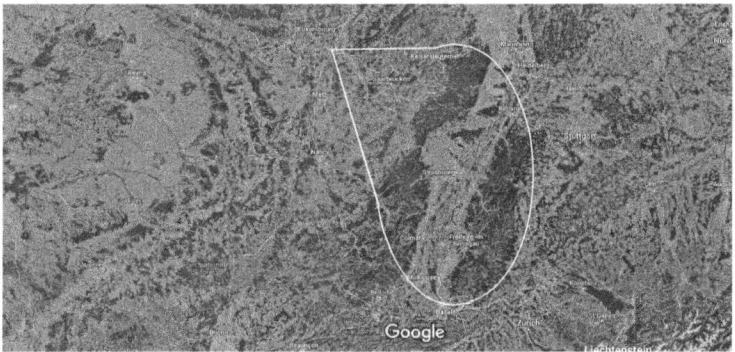

Figure 5.4 Satellite view of the France-Germany borderlands within the region
Credit: Google

French *département* of Moselle, Bas-Rhin and Haut-Rhin, which since 2016 are joined up within the extended administrative region of Grand-Est.[1]

Topographically, the upper part of the border is characterised by plateaus and hilly forests to the west, which get higher towards the east due to the presence of the northern part of the Vosges Mountains. The lower part of the border follows the course of the Rhine, which, along with the tectonic collapse of the zone situated between the Vosges Mountains and the Black Forest, contributed to the formation of a vast area of lowlands.

Whilst the German nation state was constructed according to the "'cultural model" in which the nation is seen as shaping the territory, France is based on the "State model" in which the territory is seen as shaping the nation. Whilst Germany developed as a federation, France was constructed as a centralised country with a strong State. In France, the notion of "natural borders" was promoted as a principle for the establishment and protection of the national territory using waterways and topographical features (FOUCHER, 2009). In the northern and northeastern parts of the territory where the topography did not offer the same characteristics, a series of fortresses were built by engineer and architect Vauban between 1665 and 1707. The part of French borders which proportionately received the largest number of constructions is that which extends from the North Sea to the triple border between France, Germany and Switzerland as it is situated today.

5.2 Historical contextualisation

The current shape of this border dates back to 1945, when, at the end of the Second World War, France recovered the regions of Alsace and Moselle which had been annexed to Germany in 1940 with the Franco-German armistice. This was the end of a history of shifts in the territorial and political affiliation of a region which has historically played the role of a buffer zone between France and Germany. The main historical events which affected the location of the border and the affiliation of the borderlands will be presented hereafter, not with the intention of providing a full historical analysis of the region but in general terms in order to provide context. As it is not considered relevant to draw the full history of the borderlands, this contextualisation starts from the 18th of January 1871 with the creation of the German Empire, since which the border has changed positions four times. Additionally, Table 5.1 gives a brief overview of the alternating political and territorial affiliation of the region which goes back further in time.

Table 5.1 Timeline of the political and territorial affiliations of the region

Timeframe	Political affiliation	State framework
1st century BC–5th century AD	Roman (Celtic and Germanic)	Roman framework
5th century–10th century AD	Germanic	Merovingians Carolingians
10th century–17th century AD	Germanic	Holy Roman Germanic Empire
17th century AD–1870	French	France (monarchy, republic)
1870–1918	German	2nd German Empire
1918–1940	French	France (republic)
1940–1945	German	Germany: Third Reich
1945–	French	France (republic)

With the signature of the Frankfurt Treaty on the 10th of May 1871 following the French defeat in the Franco-Prussian War, the following areas became part of Germany: the entire Lower Rhine, most of Upper Rhine as well as 75% of the Moselle territory.[2] These territories had previously belonged to the Holy Roman Germanic Empire and had changed geopolitical spheres for the first time in the 17th century following the Thirty Years' War, when they had been progressively integrated to France.

France recovered the territories following the First World War, in practice in 1918 and officially in 1920 with the Versailles Treaty. The borderline went back to its previous position and from the 1930s was accompanied by two defensive lines made up of fortifications and obstacles aiming to secure the border: the Maginot line on the French side and the Siegfried line on the German side.

With the French capitulation in the Second World War, the territories of Alsace and Moselle were integrated into German administration. Though this change was not included in the armistice signed on the 22nd of June 1940, the transfer happened in practice and the territory remained under German authority until the liberation of the region in 1945 by allied troops. Differently from other French territories which were occupied by Nazi Germany,

Alsace and Moselle were incorporated within German political and institutional structures as well as submitted to German legislation.

The position of the border as well as the political and territorial affiliation of the region have remained unchanged since 1945, except for minor changes in the delineation of the borderline which were made through an amicable settlement in 1983 in the Warndt Forest.

The now German Land of Saarland was also affected by various geopolitical changes as well as French and international influence in three phases in the 19th and 20th centuries. Firstly, it was temporarily a French department from 1801 to 1815. It was then administered by the League of Nations from 1920 following the First World War, and France was given the control of its coal mines. This lasted until 1935 when a referendum was organised, and over 90% of the population voted in favour of reintegration within Germany rather than France. Finally, following the Second World War, it was included in the French occupation zone (1945–1947), then constituted as an independent state under French Protectorate (1947–1950), recognised as an independent territory and integrated within the Council of Europe (1950–1956) and only fully integrated as the 10th land of the Federal Republic of Germany in 1957.

5.3 Demographic, economic and cultural contextualisation

In relation to French borders and their organisation, it is worth making the following general points. There is no clearly defined border strip. Some parts of the border are regulated based on a special status of "border zone" whilst others aren't. Some border strips are defined as corresponding to a certain number of kilometres from the dividing line whilst others include entire regions if they are situated by the border. In the case of the Franco-German border, the strip is defined as including 30 km on the German side, 20 km on the French side, as well as the entire *départements* of Upper Rhine, Lower Rhine and Moselle.

Economic activity in the region is mostly centred around the following sectors: agriculture (grains, beetroot and potato, amongst others), cattle breeding, wine production, wood and paper production, automotive and machinery industry, pharmaceutical industry and tourism (linked mostly to urban spaces, culture and heritage, nature and sports, and gastronomy).

Within the entire French territory, residents who cross a border every day to work in the neighbouring country are estimated at 276,000. This is the result of the higher number of available jobs in some neighbouring countries as well as of higher rates of pay. The main centres around which these cross-border networks are established are the following: Saarbrücken, Basel, Geneva and Luxembourg (FOUCHER, 2009).

The population in the French Grand Est region in general is decreasing, due to a combination of decreasing economic activity, negative net migration,

96 Cultural governance in the France-Germany borderlands

ageing population and low birth rates. However, the areas which diverge from this general tendency are those situated around urban centres in the borderlands, as they are connected to the urban and economic centres of the neighbouring countries. This generates higher income levels and thus makes the areas more attractive (GRAND EST, 2017).

As demonstrated in Figure 5.5, demographic density is higher in territories situated immediately along the borderline than in the spaces situated slightly further inside each territory. This higher density is especially visible in the lower part of the border, along the course of the Rhine around the cities of Strasbourg, Colmar, Freiburg im Breisgau, Mulhouse and Basel.[3]

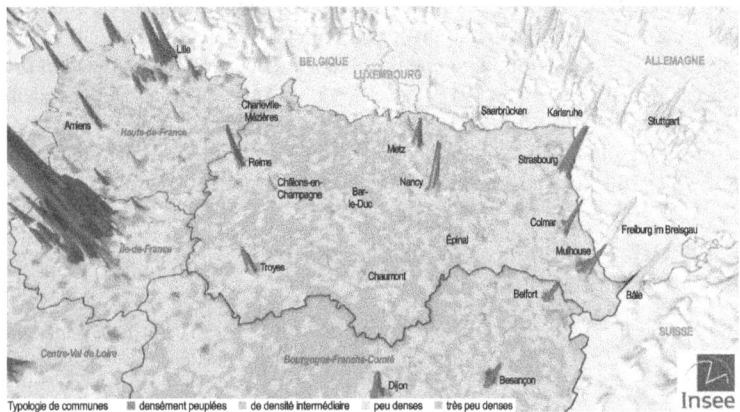

Figure 5.5 Demographic density in the Grand Est and bordering regions
Credit: EuroGraphics – INSEE (Institut national de la statistique et des études économiques), 2016

Within the French-German borderlands, this study focuses on two border urban centres[4]: firstly, the centre composed of Strasbourg (France) and Kehl (Germany); secondly, the centre composed of Huningue, Saint Louis[5] (France), Weil am Rhein (Germany) and Basel (Switzerland). The first (Strasbourg-Kehl) is composed of two discontinuous municipalities including a large city and a small town, whilst the other (Saint Louis-Weil am Rhein-Basel) is composed of a continuous urban centre (DUBOIS, 2019) (Figures 5.6 and 5.7).

This configuration is similar to our choice of cities in the Brazil-Uruguay borderlands, which includes a centre composed of two discontinuous municipalities (Jaguarão-Rio Branco) and another composed of a continuous urban area (Santana do Livramento-Rivera).

Based on the most recent census data for the two cities,[6] whilst Strasbourg's population is of 293,538 inhabitants,[7] Kehl's is of 33,551 inhabitants.[8] The cross-border urban centre of Basel includes 30,501 inhabitants in the

Cultural governance in the France-Germany borderlands 97

Strasbourg-Kehl, Saint Louis-Weil am Rhein-Basel and other main twin cities at the border between France and Germany

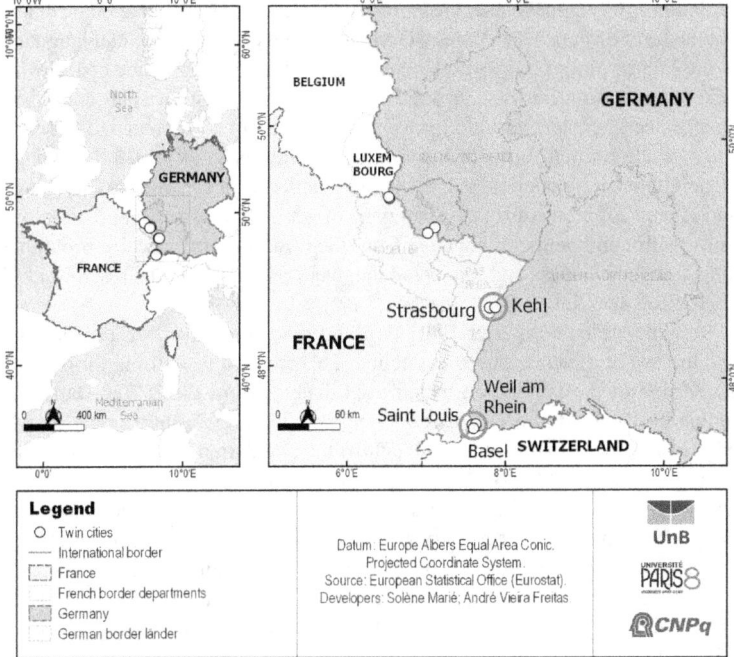

Figure 5.6 Strasbourg-Kehl, Saint Louis-Weil am Rhein-Basel and other main twin cities at the border between France and Germany

Credit: André Vieira Freitas (cartography) and Solène Marié

Figure 5.7 Photographs illustrating the continuous urban centre in Saint Louis-Weil am Rhein-Basel. Integrated public transport map (a); border street between Basel and Saint Louis (b).

Credit: Solène Marié

French part,[9] 28,828 inhabitants in the German part[10] and 173,863 inhabitants in the Swiss part.[11]

In terms of language use, the landscape has significantly changed throughout the last 50 years. Even though German has never been an official language in the French part of the borderlands since 1945, it has in practice historically held an important position through the use of both high German and Alsacian dialects in their various forms. However, though German is the reference for the written forms of local Alsacian dialects as well as the language of neighbouring countries[12], it holds the position of an exogenous language and is seen simultaneously as a language of geographical and linguistic proximity with neighbours, a language from the past, an economically profitable language for business and a rejected language (HUCK; BOTHOREL-WITZ; GEIGER-JAILLET, 2007).

In generations born after 1940, written French took over written German and the use of dialects started to decline. This resulted in a strong drop in the proportion of the population which used dialects from the 1970s. Data presented by Huck, Bothorel-Witz and Geiger-Jaillet (2007) shows that knowledge of local dialects went from 84.7% of the population in 1962 to 74.7% of the population in 1979, to 62% of the population in 1998. In 1998, division by age shows that within the 18–24 age range, the percentage of fluent speakers is of 22%, whilst that of non-speakers is of 63%; in the 65+ age range, the percentage of fluent speakers is of 79%, whilst that of non-speakers is of 16%.

The decline was especially strong in large cities in the French part of the borderlands, in which dialect use by the population born in 1980 was just over 15% in 1999.[13] Therefore, it can generally be said that the decline in the use of Alsacian is a phenomenon which is felt the most in young and urban populations, whilst the populations who maintain its use are mostly elder and rural.

In the Basel region, the linguistic landscape is even more plural. In the French part of the urban centre, most inhabitants speak French, but a portion of the population speaks Alsacian. In the German part, Standard German[14] is spoken jointly to Swabian, a dialect from Baden-Württemberg (DUBOIS, 2019). In the Swiss part, the main language is Swiss German, alongside Standard German. Amongst the languages mentioned, the Alsacian and Swabian dialects are both linguistically close to German Swiss. Additionally, as well as facing France to the northwest and Germany to the northeast, the city and canton of Basel are also connected internally to the French-speaking Swiss canton of Jura to the southwest. All these factors render linguistic plurality particularly vivid in this part of the borderlands (Figure 5.8).

As a general tendency, the results of the 2005 referendum on the European Constitution project demonstrate mixed feelings in relation to European integration in French border regions. Amongst the 19 border region districts[15] which existed at the time, the project was only approved in two of them: Bas-Rhin (56%) and Haute Savoie (54%). Voting at the municipality level also demonstrates a higher-than-average approval of the project in the border area of the Bas-Rhin

Figure 5.8 Street in Saint Louis
Credit: Solène Marié

district and at the Franco-Swiss border. Results above 50% at the local level were obtained in the following municipalities: Lille, Bayonne, Thionville, Annemasse, Barcelonette, Farney-Voltaire, Saint-Julien-en-Genevois, Mulhouse and the border municipalities of Strasbourg (where approval reached 62%) and Saint Louis (where it reached 53%) (FOUCHER, 2009). The figures from the last two cities demonstrate largely above-average support for the project in the French border cities with Germany which were chosen for analysis in this research.

5.4 Cultural governance in the borderlands: institutional context and cooperation

As theatre director and actor Giorgio Strehler comically expresses it, "Europe cannot be only about cows and olives. Europe needs culture, or it won't be" (GREGORI, 1988, p. 89). In this section, we will briefly present the main programmes and institutions which are associated with cultural policies in the France-Germany borderlands. The intention here is not to make a comprehensive inventory and description[16] but rather to focus on these programmes and institutions' role within the cultural networks in the borderlands and on actors' relations to them.

To support cross-border integration and the development of borderlands, the European Union (EU) created a programme dedicated specifically to cross-border cooperation. Created in 1990, the INTERREG programme is currently in its sixth cycle of activity: Interreg I (1990–1993), Interreg II (1994–1999), Interreg III (2000–2006), Interreg IV (2007–2013), Interreg V (2014–2020) and Interreg Europe (2021–2027).

Originally a simple communitarian initiative, INTERREG became in the 2014–2020 cycle one of the main objectives of the EU Cohesion Policy, gaining the new name of European Territorial Cooperation. The programme addresses various policy areas in borderlands and has throughout its years of existence offered support to a number of cultural projects. Depending on the programme cycles, the latter have had access to a special line of funding or, when it didn't exist, have been submitted to another line which could encompass cultural projects.

The underlying logic of this type of initiative is the following, as summarised by Martins (2007, p. 134):

> It can be argued that the process which leads to integration within "smaller" units of institutional convergence, similarly to the communities which constitute Latin-American societies, without negating their specificities and maintaining their capacity for coordination, contributes both to the subjective and collective self-affirmation and to the "bottom-up" institutionalisation of the social and cultural legitimacy of regional blocks.

With regard to culture, EU Member States did not immediately trust the regional block to get involved in these issues. Only in the 1992 Maastricht Treaty was an article included for the first time on the topic of the cultural competences of the European Union. Even so, these remain very limited, complementary to the actions of Member States and strictly framed by the principle of subsidiarity[17]. This reluctance is characteristic of the entire cultural sector with the exception of the audiovisual industry which, given its economic dimension and large audience, was considered a priority sector for EU action from the late 1980s (AUTISSIER, 2006). Furthermore, cultural policies and the structuring of the cultural sector differ largely from one Member State to another, and this complexifies the creation of unified policies and programmes at EU level.

The first large-scale EU programme geared toward the funding of cultural projects was launched in 1996 under the name of KALEIDOSCOPE. The "Culture 2000" programme followed, with a cycle of activity which ran from 2000 to 2006. It was thereafter maintained for another cycle of six years (2007–2013) under the name of "Culture". In the most recent cycle (2014–2020), the former Culture, MEDIA and MEDIA Mundus Programmes were fused and became the Creative Europe programme (2021–2027).

Culture 2000 and the subsequent Culture programme focused on the development of a common cultural space for the European population by promoting cooperation between artists, producers, cultural networks, public cultural institutions as well as other partners, but culture professionals expressed disappointment:

> In terms of official discourse, culture is definitely presented as a priority, or even one of the four "pillars" of the organisation. But in terms of

real priorities, namely those which are budgeted, cultural cooperation has become peripheral. [...] the European Union and the Council of Europe [...] have been able to develop neither strategies nor programmes which met the various cultural cooperation actors' expectations and the needs of European construction.

(WEBER, 2007, p. 98)

A 2004 study conducted by Relais Culture Europe[18] highlighted the programme's main strengths and shortcomings. The way the programme is designed resembles more that of a service than of a cultural subsidy programme: the budget file is very complicated; the commission focuses more on the management of the projects and on the number of European partners than on their content; the artistic content of the project is barely given space to; and if the project leader were to fail in the fulfilment of an engagement, the payment of yet unpaid committed amounts could be cancelled, whilst paid amounts could have to be reimbursed. Support for projects does not appear to be based on their artistic appreciation but rather on criteria relating to management: the number and diversity of partners involved, as well as the ability to carry out the project originally planned (AUTISSIER, 2006).

In its most recent form as the Creative Europe programme, this funding stream continues to generate criticism from cultural actors on a number of points. Firstly, the form of the project presented for funding remains more important than its substance: the important issue is the creation of perennial management structures rather than the quality of the project. Secondly, programme aims and criteria are seen as complex: a cultural professional taking part in a presentation of European cultural programmes[19] complains about the necessity to "tweak the project to match it with a programme objective and its specific features". Thirdly, there are entry barriers for applications as applicants are required to have existed for a minimum of two years, have significant financial reserves and cannot include a fee for the work generated by the application process into the project budget. Fourthly, the number of available programmes and unclear communication from the European Commission make it complex for often understaffed cultural organisations to navigate the funding opportunities: another participant says, "We don't have an overall idea of the programmes and we don't have the time to read them all".

Due to quantitative thinking around the choice of partners, management-led rather than quality-led evaluation of the projects as well as heavy bureaucratic processes, Autissier (2006) warns against the "relative marginalisation of artists in the European cooperation process" which is "not necessarily without consequences on the involvement of the artists themselves in the European space".

According to Perrin (2013), most structural EU funding to cultural projects comes from European Territorial Cooperation programmes, such as Interreg. In this case, cultural actions are managed within institutional structures

102 *Cultural governance in the France-Germany borderlands*

which are specifically framed to correspond to EU funding specificities. This is the case of many euroregions, a term used to describe cross-border cooperation initiatives of various types between subnational governments located on both sides of a European border, for the pursuit of joint aims and projects (PERRIN, 2015). In this context, cultural actions within euroregions are used for differentiation, whilst including them within administrative set-ups which are unlikely to allow for future autonomy of the project outside of the latter (PERRIN, 2013).

In the context of the French regional reform of 2016, the newly born Grand Est region conducted a survey on the cross-border activities of cultural actors from the region.[20] Though the design of the survey is based on a notion of "cross-border" actions which encompasses all activities developed across borders, therefore international activities in general, it nonetheless offers useful data in the context of this research. Though the region shares borders with four countries (Belgium, Luxembourg, Germany and Switzerland), nearly 80% of projects developed by respondents were in partnership with a German organisation (GRAND EST, 2019).

Also, the results of the survey show that, in a country strongly oriented towards public funding of cultural activities, only 50.4% of cross-border projects had received funding, whilst 49.6% had received none.

Amongst projects having received funding, whilst 60% are supported by the region and nearly 60% by other local authorities, the EU arrives in third position with an existing support to 40% of the projects (the other three types of funding – sponsorship, foundation and crowfunding – all individually constitute less than 15% of the funding) (GRAND EST, 2019).

However, the significance of UE support within all sources of funding differs widely from one cultural sector to another. In the heritage, digital and audiovisual sectors, the EU is the first funder, followed by local authorities and finally by different types of private funding. In the cinema, visual arts, publishing, music and performing arts sectors, the EU is the third funder after the Grand Est region and other local authorities, and before private funding. Within this category, visual arts benefits, nonetheless, from significantly more funding from the EU than other sectors, even though it is proportionately lower than funding from the Grand Est (first source of funding) and other local authorities (second source of funding).

This survey also provides data on obstacles to cross-border cooperation presented by the participants. The following categories of obstacles were included in the results (from the most frequently mentioned to the least frequently mentioned): insufficient financial means (over 55%), insufficient staffing/administrative capacity (over 50%), difficulties in understanding the administrative and logistics set-up (40%), language barrier, lack of information, difficulties in understanding the institutional context, difficulties in understanding the organization of the sector, difficulties in understanding

Cultural governance in the France-Germany borderlands 103

business models, difficulties linked to cultural understanding, insufficient economic appeal, other difficulties and insufficient artistic appeal.

The fact that 50% of projects are set up with no funding and that actors mention insufficient financial means as the first obstacle is coherent, though it shows that this obstacle does not totally hinder the development of projects for the 50% that take place anyway (though possibly on a smaller scale). The other two mentioned obstacles (insufficient staffing/administrative capacity and difficulty in understanding the administrative and logistics set-up) are in line with the complaints regarding complexities in access to EU funding presented previously and can also refer to difficulties with administrative set-ups with multiple layers of funding within one's own country as well as in the neighbouring country. However, responses to other questions seem to point in the direction of a difficulty in cooperating with a distinct national context: 35% of respondents mention a language barrier, followed by difficulties in understanding the institutional context, the organization of the sector and the business models.

Notes

1. Prior to the French regional reform which took place in 2016, Moselle was part of the Lorraine region, whilst Bas-Rhin and Haut-Rhin were part of the Alsace region.
2. According to administrative divisions of the time.
3. The city of Basel is situated in Switzerland, but it is the main city of the trinational pole at the triple border between France, Germany and Switzerland. Therefore, it is customary to refer to the junction of Huningue/Saint-Louis (France), Weil am Rhein (Germany) and Basel (Switzerland) by referring to the latter.
4. The term "twin border cities", largely used in literature on South American border cities, is not used in this book in the context of European cities as it is not generally seen in literature and in order to avoid confusion with the programme of city twinning in the European Union.
5. Though the municipality which is geographically located at the triple border is that of Huningue, it is a small town of 7,213 inhabitants which is part of the municipality (*communauté d'agglomération*) of Saint-Louis. As the largest town in the grouping of towns (*intercommunalité*) with 21,777 inhabitants, Saint-Louis gives its name to the municipality. Hereafter, the name of Saint-Louis is used to refer to the French municipality situated at the triple border.
6. Population data included in this paragraph, as it comes from three different countries and thus three different census systems, is unfortunately not from the same years. However, the most recent figures were included for each case in order to give the most up-to-date information. The proportions of population living on each side of the border have not changed significantly throughout recent years.
7. INSEE 2020 census data, which is the most recent available.
8. German 2011 census data, which is the most recent available.
9. Taking into account the towns of Huningue and Saint-Louis and based on 2020 census data from INSEE.
10. Based on 2011 census data.
11. 2020 Swiss population data, which is the most recent available.
12. Germany and Germanophone Switzerland.

13 Taking into account the fact that transmission of Alsacian takes place essentially within the family and thus can occur at a young age.
14 Hochdeutsch.
15 *Départements*.
16 In line with the asymmetrical nature of this study, in which this second case serves as a shadow case in order to provide a counterpoint to the first one.
17 Which "seeks to safeguard the ability of the Member States to take decisions and action and authorises intervention by the Union when the objectives of an action cannot be sufficiently achieved by the Member States, but can be better achieved at Union level".
18 French public agency for European cultural innovation which gives support to cultural actors and researchers in terms of project development and cooperation networks. Now serves as Creative Europe desk in France.
19 Field notes from observation conducted by the author at the workshop "Atelier de présentation des programmes européens" within the event "LabEurope". Le Shadok, Strasbourg, 10/05/2019.
20 Interview with Mischa Schmelter, cross-border and European cultural policy officer, Région Grand Est, Direction de la Culture, du Patrimoine et de la Mémoire. Conducted by the author by telephone, 21/06/2019.

References

AUTISSIER, Anne-Marie. Un théâtre sans commissaires. **Etudes Théâtrales**. v. 3, n. 37, pp. 118–125, 2006.

DUBOIS, Y. **Frontières et mobilité au quotidien. Modes de vie dans l'agglomération trinationale de Bâle**. Neuchâtel: Editions Alphil-Presses Universitaires Suisses, 2019.

FOUCHER, Michel. **Obsessão por fronteiras**. São Paulo: Radical Livros. Tradução de Cecília Lopes, 2009. [Original title: L'Obsession des frontières].

GRAND EST. Direction de la communication. **Diagnostic territorial du Grand Est. Synthèse du diagnostic général du schéma régional d'aménagement, de développement durable et d'égalité des territoires**, Novembre 2017.

GRAND EST. **Synthèse des résultats de l'enquête relative à l'activité transfrontalière des acteurs culturels du Grand Est**, Juillet 2019.

GREGORI, Maria Grazia. De l'utopie au projet. Théâtre en Europe. n. 18, pp. 82–89, 1988.

HUCK, D. [coord.]; BOTHOREL-WITZ, A.; GEIGER-JAILLET, A. **L'Alsace et ses langues. Eléments de description d'une situation sociolinguistique en zone frontalière**. Report for Language Bridges, a Sub-theme Working Group of the Interreg IIIC Project Change on Borders, 2007.

PERRIN, T. La gouvernance culturelle dans les eurorégions: enjeux et dynamiques. **Eurolimes. Journal of the Institute for Euroregional Studies Oradea-Debrecen**, v. 16, pp. 63–78, 2013.

PERRIN, T. Creative regions on a European cross-border scale: Policy issues and development perspectives. **European Planning Studies**, v. 23, n. 12, pp. 2423-2437 2015.

6 Cultural ecosystems in borderlands

6.1 Multidimensional analysis of cultural ecosystems in borderlands

6.1.1 Places: the topography of culture

In the context of the multi-sited ethnographic study conducted for this research, the first phase of the fieldwork consisted in the carrying out of non-systematic observation, informal conversations and visits of cultural spaces in the entire borderlands, in the two cases, as well as in large cities connected to the borderlands in the Brazilian context (Porto Alegre and Pelotas). The second phase of the fieldwork was carried out in selected locations: the border twin cities of Jaguarão-Río Branco, Santana do Livramento-Rivera, Strasbourg-Kehl and Basel-Saint Louis-Weil am Rhein. Subjective data was collected through in-depth semi-structured interviews, and objective data was collected when available from public administration as well as from interviewees.

The first phase of fieldwork indicated a stronger rooting of borderland cultural networks in border twin cities than in municipalities situated further inside national territories within the border regions, though the latter are not exempt of involvement in these issues and of activities related to borderland culture.[1] However, observations corroborated the fact that it is in cities situated by the borderline that border culture, cultural production and cultural networks could be felt most intensely.

Bento (2015, p. 51) argues that, as a practice linked to everyday life and even survival, border culture is situated in border twin cities, especially in conurbations:

> the reasons for local integration among the populations of such conurbated border cities are above all factual, material reasons. In other words, such integration is not a consequence of (ideal) integration projects, it is not the result of a metaphysics of integration. Rather, it stems from the absence of geographical accidents, which allows a continuous flow of people and goods and is the result of the factual need for economic survival of the

DOI: 10.4324/9781003413400-6

binational populations of these border cities that are far from the administrative centres of their respective states of belonging.

Material aspects can also affect local cultural practices, for example through the access to radios from the neighbouring country (MORAES, 2002) as well as TV channels, both mentioned by many interviewees in Brazil-Uruguay border cities as having shaped a familiarity with the neighbouring country's media and a habit of listening to its traditional musical styles.

In general terms, cities also constitute the most privileged spaces for cultural production based on their higher concentration of cultural actors, cultural institutions and, in some cases, cultural capital. They are viewed as the ultimate cultural and creative spaces (SAEZ, 2004) which enjoy more advantages than other sub-national governments in terms both of cultural production and of cultural local and international policy (ZAMORANO; MORATÓ, 2014).

In Jesus's (2017) study of Brazilian cities' cultural policy presented previously, one of the five factors presented as contributing to the development of an assertive municipal cultural paradiplomacy is the interdependence of the city, a factor which is highly developed in border twin cities. In the EU context, "urban networks form the backbone of Euroregions" (PERRIN, 2015, p. 6). Thus, focus was placed on border twin cities in the research.

6.1.2 Practices: the cultural actions

Subsequently, a number of culture-related projects which were identified as key in their relation to the Brazil-Uruguay borderlands will be presented in order to serve as the basis for the presentation of the nature of activists' contribution to the cultural networks in the Brazil-Uruguay borderlands. Other projects will be mentioned in a lesser amount of detail in this subsection and the subsequent ones, and parallels will be drawn with the France-Germany borderlands in order to bring a counterpoint and depth to the analysis.

The first project is the Fronteras Culturales/Fronteiras Culturais movement,[2] which is also the most wide-ranging in terms of space as, though it stems from Santana do Livramento-Rivera and is mainly rooted in the Brazil-Uruguay borderlands, its activity extends over all of Brazil's borderlands. Its networks were found to be the densest and the most agile in terms of articulation between actors in the twin cities studied.[3] It was officially created in 2010, a year after the group initiated its activities[4] around the aim of "thinking the Latin American from the border",[5] grounded in empirical actions and valuing pre-existing projects as well as the borderlands as a space. It is led by Ricardo Almeida, project manager in the sectors of ICT and cultural integration. The movement gathers researchers, public agents, artists, producers and cultural collectives around the aim of creating "cultural integration corridors"[6] (ALMEIDA; DORFMAN, 2017, p. 149) in the borderlands, based on the cultural spaces, themes and biomes which can be encountered in sub-sections of the borderlands. It considers that borderland cultural integration projects

Cultural ecosystems in borderlands 107

are those which meet three criteria: (1) cultural integration as a theme, (2) creation of work and wages on both sides of an international border and (3) binational participation from civil society (ALMEIDA; DORFMAN, 2017).

The main participations of the movement to political actions in favour of culture and cultural networks in the borderlands are exposed concisely in Table 6.1.

Table 6.1 Main participations of the Fronteras Culturales movement to political actions in favour of cultural production, policy and networks in the borderlands

Year	Name of document/event	Role played by Fronteras Culturales	Main results
12 July 2010	Border letter[15]	Participation in the elaboration, jointly with local mayors and governors. Letter submitted to Uruguayan and Brazilian presidents.[16]	- Affirmation of culture as "one of the cohesive pillars for sustainable development, as it aims to promote self-esteem and the feeling of belonging, the recognition and appreciation of the historical and cultural heritage of the border communities". - Claim that "it is important and urgent to strengthen the cultural actions of the border communities, as well as to expand and democratise the access to services as well as tangible and intangible goods, cultural policies and actions, and to strengthen the cultural economy, capacities and local knowledge".
2011	Cultural Intentions Protocol[17]	Document signed by Uruguayan and Brazilian presidents[18] acknowledging the demands presented in the border letter.	- Document was recognised within Mercosul forums. - More explicit recognition from Uruguayan than Brazilian federal institutions.
2013	Brazil-Uruguay Border Cultural Integration calendar	Elaboration of the calendar in collaboration with local universities, local consulates and border committees.	Elaboration of an explicit calendar of cultural events in the borderlands which celebrated border culture and/or cooperation between cultural actors in the borderlands.
23 January 2016	Participation in World Social Forum in Porto Alegre	Organisation of a one-day event bringing together artists, producers, collectives and researchers to discuss borderland cultural integration.	- Participation in a large-scale international event. - Increasing visibility of the issues.

Credit: Solène Marié

Almeida points to the stronger support to the movement and its actions from Uruguayan institutions than Brazilian ones, the latter's support being more moral than tangible[7] (Figure 6.1)

(a)   (b)

Figure 6.1 Marketing documents from the Brazil-Uruguay Cultural Integration Calendar

Credit: Archive of the Fronteras Culturales movement

The second selected event is the Binational Festival of Oeno-gastronomy and products from the Pampa,[8] led by Jussara Dutra, ex-Chef of the Piratini Palace[9] restaurant, now researcher and curator of the festival. In 2011, Dutra was nominated by Tarso Genro[10] as Chef of the Piratini Palace, position which previously had always been held by men from the military and had been carried out with no specific rooting in regional cuisine. She suggested that the Palace become, in this context, a location for the promotion of traditional cuisine from the Rio Grande do Sul as intangible heritage. Due to the absence of previous research or actions on this topic, she launched a large research project involving historians, nutritionists, an anthropologist and students in order to gather data from elderly people, restaurants and traditional food producers. The research project which lasted from 2001 to 2014 as well as the first edition of the festival in 2014 were conducted exclusively with Rio Grande do Sul state public funding.

The border conurbation of Santana do Livramento-Rivera was chosen to host the event, and a significant emphasis was put on regional food traditions from the borderlands as well as on the binational aspect of the project. As stated clearly by Dutra[11] (2018), "it was impossible to conceive any project here at the border without it being binational"; "everything we do in the festival has to be binational".

The aim of presenting the results of the research project in various formats and channels was not achieved as funding for the project was interrupted with the change in state government in 2015. The 2015 and 2016 editions were supported by the Rivera townhall and state government.[12] From 2017, local businesses and trade unions added their support to the festival budget. Finally, the festival received support from the Lei Rouanet tax incentive mechanism for the first time in its 2018 edition. The festival, alongside its activities

Cultural ecosystems in borderlands 109

strictly focused on gastronomy, also includes other cultural activities around photography and cinema as well as social activities, all of them largely focused on the binational and cross-border location of the festival (Figure 6.2).[13]

Figure 6.2 Binational Festival of Oeno-gastronomy and products from the Pampa: visual identity

Credit: Fronte(i)ra - Festival Binacional de Enogastronomia

The third event is the Binational Book Fair[14] in Santana do Livramento-Rivera, created in 2010 by the Marco Zero bookshop and led by its joint owner Artur Montanari. Despite the initial idea of conducting this Fair in the International Park which is crossed by the border in the middle of the two cities, this was not possible in the first edition and the event was transferred to the Casa de Cultura in Santana do Livramento. In 2011, based on the support of the Brazilian local consul in Rivera,[19] the transfer to the International Park was possible. The Fair continued in 2012 and 2013 with success, based on significant help from the local consul.[20] However, in 2014, the combination of an interruption in local consulate support and personal conflicts within the organising team led to an interruption of the Fair, which did not happen again. As pointed out by Montanari,[21]

> it depends a lot on the initiative of specific people who lead some processes. If these people are absent or they are missing, I think the tendency is that things start to go wrong, it starts slowing down, and then it ends up collapsing. That's what happened to our Fair.

Changes in people affect processes with regard to cultural activists both within civil society and within government. As shown in the case of the Oeno-gastronomy Festival presented previously, changes in government can mark the end of a funding or support stream. Montanari also points out this difficulty, regarding a free mini-library project in various locations in the city:

> It worked really well. And there was no continuity because the government changed. Then the other government was not interested and as it is a public space we depended on them, on the consent of the municipality. So the library ended.

6.1.3 People: the actors

The first actors who are highlighted for their importance in cross-border cultural network processes are the social elite. They are mentioned for their crucial role both as project leaders and as audiences.

As evidenced previously through the analysis of the Mercosul's role in initiating actions in the sectors of cultural and borderland integration in the Brazil-Uruguay borderlands, the latter's role is shown to be limited and its main contribution to be symbolic. This is in consonance with the situation in other South American borderlands, as stated by Amilhat Szary (2010, pp. 11–12):

> It is difficult [...] to assert that the momentum for cross-border regional development that can be seen across much of Latin America's borders is a direct result of the integration processes underway. It is part of a much more general awareness of the value of territories and the importance of working on local / global relationships to successfully secure a place within globalisation. In practice, there are not so many specific cooperation instruments in place.

Based on a peripheral location, weaknesses in institutional and political representation, as well as a historical context of regionalisation of politics (CLEMENTE, 2010), local elites took on a role in the vocalisation of issues affecting their territory. Between the 1980s and the 1990s throughout the South American subcontinent, projects were born out of these influent local groups' initiative, through a bottom-up dynamic based on local resources and pragmatic necessity for survival (AMILHAT SZARY, 2010).

This configuration is especially visible in the cultural sector in Santana do Livramento-Rivera, which is mainly built upon activism. Montanari[22] points out that those who lead cultural initiatives in the borderlands in Santana do Livramento are

> "essentially civil society and the agents themselves. There are few governmental initiatives. You have the question of the Farroupilha week, which concerns the entire state, the roots of the *gaúcho*. All this is strong here. [...] One of the few people doing cultural production here who successfully raises funds is the person working on folk culture. [...] Because it's about the *gaúcho* theme, he can do it. But for the others, it's difficult. It depends a lot on the initiative of the cultural agents who are making culture."

Thus, the only actor who is seen as managing to secure support from public authorities is the person whose cultural actions are linked to a wider topic involving other regions beyond the borderlands.

Additionally, populations who are identified as connecting to the borderlands and to the binational culture which is present locally, as well as to cultural events as audiences, are the regional elite. As pointed out by Palermo,[23]

> no one enters my museum, but in a musical show [...] 5000, 6000, 7000 people go. [...] Some issues are more elite consumption than popular consumption, even if those you are watching in these expressions can have a low income. Yes, but those who enjoy it are not low-income groups, they are the elite. Low-income people do other things, [...] are in other styles, not in these. [...] Border culture is a popular culture, not an elite culture.

As a result of both these cultural preferences and a concentration of cultural events in the centre, audiences tend to be the same in the different events and tend to be higher income inhabitants from the city centres.[24] They also depend a lot on relations between local artists who, though they are still searching for a way of structuring their actions as a network, demonstrate close relations and a knowledge of the work of the main artistic figures of the region.[25] As pointed out by visual artist and arts teacher Dionéia de Macedo,[26]

> We need to fight hard to create something that brings an audience, you know? [...] As artists, we get together more, exchange more, for example if they do an exhibition there, all the Brazilians go, if a Brazilian does one here all the Uruguayans come, we support each other.

Another important role played by actors is that of political elites and networks. Firstly, as pointed out previously, Border Committees of twin cities were the initiators of fundamental local political representation and action from the 1990s and, though their actions are not constant and sometimes suffer interruptions, they are still important actors in local political networks.

Secondly, the importance of the local Brazilian and Uruguayan consulates in border cities is highlighted by many actors in both Santana do Livramento-Rivera and Jaguarão-Rio Branco as being fundamental to the organisation of cultural events. Britos[27] points out that "the mistake" committed in Jaguarão was having recently tried to interact with ministries rather than with consulates, which enable cultural actors to "skip a few levels" in the bureaucracy and thus "obtain something".

Rodrigo Segovia, Culture and Tourism Secretary in Jaguarão from 2017 to 2019, formulates clearly:

> as I observed, to make life easier at the border in terms of bureaucratic issues: use the consulates. Because... let's say, the consulate is politically neutral. And if the consuls get involved ... and this, let's say, is a political manoeuver that I've been able to use and is working. [...] With the one

in Porto Alegre I never talked, nor with the one in Montevideo. We talk directly with the border consulates, but the Uruguayan consulate in Brazil is the most active, by 99%.

However, when it comes to cultural actions, this relationship with consuls working in border city consulates does not appear to be based on institutional or political relationship. Rather, it appears to be based on the personality of the consul and a possible personal involvement in cultural issues. This is reinforced by Segovia's highlighting of the fact that 99% of consulate involvement stems from one of the two border consulates. The oscillations in the Binational Book Fair in Santana do Livramento-Rivera also appear to be in large part linked to the presence or absence of support from specific consuls involved in cultural issues. In the case of the Book Fair, support came from two successive consuls who had "excellent involvement in the cultural sector" and were "very open and receptive".[28]

Finally, corresponding visions between politicians in the different instances involved appears to accelerate many of the processes which led to the organisation of summits, the voting of legal documents but also the creation of cultural initiatives and the involvement in national funding programmes. This convergence is even stronger in the case of politicians from the same political group.

Table 6.2 presents all the year numbers mentioned in the interviews conducted in the Brazil-Uruguay borderlands as well as the number of times they were mentioned and the weighted percentage they represent in the total amount of words said in all the interviews.

It appears that no mentions of years prior to 2007 or after 2015 were made.[29] Also, mentions during the period going from 2009 to 2014 are much higher than in the other years, with peaks in the years 2009, 2011 and 2014. Looking at political mandates throughout this period, we can see that it corresponded to a period of convergence of political visions between Brazilian

Table 6.2 Years mentioned in the interviews in number of occurrences and weighted percentage

Word	Count	Weighted percentage
2007	69	0.01%
2008	82	0.01%
2009	417	0.08%
2010	165	0.03%
2011	621	0.11%
2012	301	0.05%
2013	289	0.05%
2014	600	0.11%
2015	126	0.02%

Credit: Produced by Solène Marié with NVivo 12

Cultural ecosystems in borderlands 113

and Uruguayan left-wing presidents, as well as of political leaders from the same Brazilian party, the Workers' Party[30] (PT).

The colouring of the years in which this political convergence existed shows that the period of more intense activity took place within these years, demonstrating the existence of a window of opportunity bold (bold in Table 6.3) between 2008 and 2014, with the strongest convergence between 2011 and 2014.

Table 6.3 Periods of left-wing government in local, state and federal governments in Brazil and Uruguay (light grey) and window of opportunity (in bold)

Year	Brazilian President	Uruguayan President	RS Governor	Jaguarão Mayor[31]
2003	Lula, PT (first mandate)	Jorge Luis Battle Ibáñez, Partido Colorado	Germano Rigotto, PMDB	Henrique Edmar Knorr Filho, PMDB
2004				
2005				
2006				
2007	Lula, PT (second mandate)	Tabaré Vázquez, Frente Amplio	Yeda Crusius, PSDB	
2008				
2009				
2010				
2011	**Dilma Rousseff, PT (first mandate)**		**Tarso Genro, PT**	Claudio Martins, PT[32]
2012				
2013		**Pepe Mujica, Frente Amplio**		
2014				
2015	Dilma Rousseff, PT (second mandate[33])		José Ivo Sartori, PMDB	
2016	Michel Temer, PMDB	Tabaré Vázquez, Frente Amplio		

Credit: Solène Marié

Finally, the third category of actors who are pointed out as playing a strong role in cross-border cultural networks are universities. Mercher, Bernardo and Silva (2018, p. 20) point out that universities "played a decisive role" in the creation of the Working Group for Border Integration within the Mercocities Network. As institutions which are more secure and governed by long-term policies in terms of funding, they appear to play the important role of maintaining initiatives alive, even in dormant form, in between more intense phases in which cultural actors are able to sustain a project, sometimes funded by a supportive government or funding stream.

In Jaguarão, the 2012 listing of the historical centre as national historical monument by the National Institute of Historic and Artistic Heritage (IPHAN) following a previous inscription by the Institute of Historical and Artistic Heritage of the Rio Grande do Sul State[34] (IPHAE) was based on the work of a professor of architecture and urbanism from the Federal University of

114 *Cultural ecosystems in borderlands*

Pelotas[35] who, through the Jaguar Project in the 1990s, led a long-term inventory of historical buildings in Jaguarão.[36] Adriana Ança[37] highlights clearly this role of universities:

> in fact, this is the thing: I think we have always been driven by universities, Universities discovered us. It was already the case in the 1990s [...]. The Federal University of Pelotas comes to Jaguarão, starts doing this work. [...] And that's where it starts, you understand? I think it is something which comes more from the University, because it has a certain connection with heritage bodies [...] So, here comes the IPHAE to Jaguarão [...], it does this inventory and lists some buildings.

Finally, as highlighted previously, a role was played by universities and researchers within the Oeno-gastronomy Festival in Santana do Livramento-Rivera in terms of collection of information and production of knowledge on the borderlands, topic which lacks research in many areas. Dutra also insists that the participation of five different universities to the festival is a "very important aspect for the question of integration".[38]

6.2 Spatial, institutional and social (re)compositions in borderland cultural ecosystems

6.2.1 *Cultural networks in the Brazil-Uruguay borderlands: parallels with the France-Germany borderlands*

Word clouds were produced based on the interviews conducted with actors from each of the borderlands. Though these are not meant for objective and precise analysis, their strength is to enable effective and easy visualisation of word frequency and relationality. They are presented in Figures 6.3 and 6.4.

The word cloud presented in Figure 6.3, unsurprisingly, highlights the centrality of the themes of culture (*cultura, culturais*); border (*fronteira*); people (*gente, pessoas, pessoal*) and the two countries Brazil and Uruguay (*Brasil, Uruguai*). The word "city" (*cidade*) as well as city names such as Jaguarão and, with lesser centrality, Pelotas are also displayed as significant within the word "cloud". However, the words "region" (*região*) and "municipality" (*municipalidade*) are less central. The words "policies" (*políticas*), "government" (*governo*), "department" (*secretaria*) and "state" (*estado*) are also present, though they are situated more towards the edge of the cloud. Finally, theatre (*teatro*), literature (*livro*) and tourism (*turismo*) appear as associated to the topic. No other specific artistic disciplines are mentioned.

In the word cloud presented in Figure 6.4, centrality is given to projects (*projets*) and actors (*acteurs*). The topics of the border (*frontière, transfrontalier, transfrontaliers, transfrontalière*) and culture (*culturels, culture, culturel, culturelles*) are also present, though slightly more peripheric. The names of the countries involved are also present (*France, Allemagne, allemand,*

Cultural ecosystems in borderlands 115

Figure 6.3 Word cloud based on interviews conducted at the Brazil-Uruguay borderlands

Credit: Produced by Solène Marié with NVivo 12

Figure 6.4 Word cloud based on interviews conducted at the France-Germany borderlands

Credit: Produced by Solène Marié with NVivo 12

116 *Cultural ecosystems in borderlands*

Suisse). The words "region" (*région*), "city/town" (*ville*) and "Strasbourg" are also present, with more centrality for the first word. The other names of cities are not visible. Finally, the lexical field of cooperation is present in words such as "cooperation" (*coopération*), "work" (*travail, travailler*), "together" (*ensemble*) and that of policies in the words "policies" (*politiques*) and "Interreg".

6.2.1.1 Favourable factors and obstacles

Tables 6.4 and 6.5 give a condensed overview of the factors which were identified in literature on the subject and through the totality of the fieldwork conducted for this research, as being favourable to the fostering of existing or past cultural projects in the borderlands, as well as those identified as constituting obstacles to their development. More detail will subsequently be given about the main factors.

Table 6.4 Factors identified as fostering existing cultural projects in the borderlands

	Brazil-Uruguay borderlands	France-Germany borderlands
PLACES	Municipalities	Municipalities
PEOPLE	Human connections	Projects led by cultural institutions rather than public administration
	Political connections	
PRACTICES: political/ institutional	Windows of opportunity	Framing of projects based on funding institutions' criteria Inclusion of culture within wider projects
PRACTICES: cultural	Cultural industries and tourism Tangible and perennial structures	Cultural and creative industries Tourism Perennial and rich structures

Credit: Solène Marié

6.2.1.2 The question of leadership

The study of the configuration of cultural projects in the Brazil-Uruguay borderlands showed the important role played by personal initiative and civil society activism, especially in the border conurbation of Santana do Livramento-Rivera. Mostly, projects depend on the strong leadership from a person who has the desire to create a cross-border project and the strength of vision to make it happen. Ricardo Almeida is the figure who is identifiable as central in order to give the necessary impulse to bring the project of the Fronteras Culturales movement to life, as well as to operate the necessary political articulation. Jussara Dutra also plays this role within the movement and festival which she created and she formulates clearly[39] the importance of the vision and leadership she brought to the project:

> SM: And what made the overcoming of this difficulty possible? What were the instrumental elements to achieve this binational aspect in the project?

Table 6.5 Factors identified as obstacles to the development of cultural projects in the borderlands

	Brazil-Uruguay borderlands	France-Germany borderlands
PLACES		
PEOPLE	Success highly dependent upon specific individuals	Lack of relations between actors and fragmented networks
	Lack of technical training	Communication/linguistic barriers
PRACTICES: political/ institutional	Bureaucratic obstacles	Difficulties in understanding administrative/cultural/ tax system in the other country
	Unstable and often short-term funding	EU funding systems difficult to navigate for small/new organisations
	Lack of coordination between different levels of government	Lack of links between institutions and artists
PRACTICES: cultural	Elite audiences	Audiences lack knowledge of artistic expressions from the other country

Credit: Solène Marié

JD: I think that... First, I would say, the fact that I was coordinating and had this as a guideline, the importance of cultural integration of this border. So I think this is fundamental, to always have someone in the leadership of the project who does not lose that guiding principle.

The connection of the project leader to the borderlands in their spatial and symbolic aspects in one way or another is also crucial. Both these leaders are from the borderlands,[40] and this factor appears as important to their protagonism both in terms of gaining the necessary respect and support needed to their enterprise, as well as through the personal relations and knowledge of the local reality that it brings.

Within the context of cultural governance in Euroregions, Perrin (2013) also points out the position of a number of actors who, in a landscape of scarcity of resources, manage to lead projects based on their better understanding of procedures as well as on their relations with decision-makers.

6.2.1.3 The windows of opportunity

Secondly, a factor which is significant in the activity of cultural networks in both borderlands is that of windows of opportunity.

In the case of the Brazil-Uruguay borderlands, a window of opportunity clearly appears to have existed for the launching of cultural projects in the borderlands from 2008 to 2014. In 2008, Brazilian federal legislative activity around the issue of borders experienced a significant peak. It is also the year of the creation of the MinC's DRI, which officialised the latter's involvement in international cultural activities jointly with the MRE. As pointed out previously, interviews conducted in the context of this research demonstrate a significant rise in mentions of years from 2009. Santana do Livramento was recognised as symbol of Brazilian integration with other Mercosul countries in 2009. The Fronteras Culturales movement, which was founded in Santana do Livramento, initiated its activities in 2010, which was the year of Pepe Mujica's election and marked the beginning of a strong convergence in visions and personalities between the presidents of Uruguay and Brazil. It was also the year in which the International Book Fair of Santana do Livramento had its first edition. Finally, with the election of a left-wing governor at the head of the Rio Grande do Sul state in 2011, Jussara Dutra was nominated chef of the Piratini Palace and initiated the research project which later led to the creation of the Oeno-gastronomic Festival. She points to the existence of this window of opportunity[41]:

> In 2013, I think it was, during Governor Tarso Genro's administration, there was a very strong impetus for cultural integration between Brazil and Uruguay [...] and Brazil and Argentina integration, right, border issues. So there was an international relations department within the government which led mediations with Uruguay and Argentina, who was [led by] Tarson Nuñez.

In the France-Germany borderlands, cultural actors are generally confronted to difficulties in securing funding for cross-border projects. Especially through EU programmes, two types of windows of opportunity can be identified. Firstly, cultural actors can tailor their projects to existing programmes which sometimes do not have a cultural section, such as the Interreg programme which, throughout its cycles, has alternated between having and not having a section for cultural projects. Secondly, they can integrate wider projects from other areas. As highlighted by Perrin (2013, p. 75),

> Culture, through its potential in terms of visibility and its high symbolic load, appears as a privileged field of action to bring "meaning" to Euroregional constructions which, because of their institutional and structural weakness, still appear as territorial cooperation experiments, "laboratories", more than actual transboundary polities, strictly speaking.

Correspondingly, in the projects led by IBA Basel which works within the scope of the Basel Trinational district, culture is seen as bringing a participative aspect to their projects linked to urbanism and architecture to "give them visibility or make them more understandable for the population".[42]

6.2.1.4 The tangible, marketable, perennial

Two elements appear to contribute to a stronger ability of cultural projects and events to be perennial in the Brazil-Uruguay borderlands and also appear as pregnant in the France-Germany borderlands.

Firstly, projects linked to the cultural and creative industries seem to ensure their survival more effectively than other cultural sectors. Most perennial festivals and groups encountered in the Brazil-Uruguay borderlands[43] were from the sectors of literature, music, gastronomy and visual arts. In a context of volatile public funding, organisers are better able to create alternative funding models based on sponsorship in the case of the loss of public funding, as it was the case for the Oeno-gastronomic Festival in Santana do Livramento-Rivera, for example.

EU funding programmes are also making a shift in this direction, as pointed out by Frédérique Chabaud[44]:

> we don't necessarily talk about projects anymore [...] we're now really talking about the creative and cultural industries. So in there you are also starting to have other players, such as design, architecture, you see? We are really starting to explore [...] the fringe, which is fundamental for culture, but at the same time increases the number of potential actors. And sometimes reduces the chances for small theatres, for small associations, for small museums which are city museums, for example.

Secondly, projects linked to a tangible structure appear to benefit from the advantages of their long-term nature as well as their potential economic impact. In Brazil, the revitalisation of Jaguarão's historical centre was funded through the Programa de Aceleração do Crescimento programme, an economic growth acceleration programme specially designed for historical cities.

EU funding is currently seeing a "strong expansion"[45] of opportunities in the heritage sector. They are in part linked to tourism, which enables value generation from tangible heritage. Previously, the 2007–2013 policy framework for EU Structural Funds already demonstrated a strong connection of cultural funding with the issues of cultural heritage and goods, tourism as well as the construction and renovation of cultural infrastructure (AUTISSIER, 2011).

Anne Poidevin[46] explains the relevance of tangibility in the case of cultural projects in borderlands, linked to the

> fact that there are physical places to see [...]. I think the most complicated thing is the somewhat virtual projects. [...] And I think that in the case of cross-border [projects], because there is a geographic proximity, it is good that there is something physical, actually. And it's easier to make it last over time, as you would expect.

6.3 The specifics of cultural ecosystems in borderlands: dynamics and processes

6.3.1 The border, between presence and absence

Word clouds produced based on words used by interviewees in the Brazil-Uruguay and France-Germany borderlands showed a strong centrality of the term "border" in the first case, whilst it was presented as less central in the second one.

Furthermore, marketing documents from the three cultural events/networks from the Brazil-Uruguay borderlands presented previously (see figures 6.1 and 6.2), whilst promoting cross-border integration, show the centrality of the border in their visual and therefore, organisational, identity. The symbolic presence of the border in these events is strong, like in everyday life in which the territory is often referred to as "the border".

In the France-Germany borderlands, the significance of the border is different. Projects appear to be more focused on Franco-German or European cooperation than on the borderlands per se,[47] and these two types of cooperation models appear similar in the sense that there would be no fundamental difference between a collaboration project involving French and German artists from Paris and Berlin or from Strasbourg and Kehl[48] (Figure 6.5)

Perrin (2013, p. 68) highlights the fact that "identity is particularly complex to handle in a cross-border context and culture can be the 'cement' which binds cooperation as much as the 'acid' which dissolves it".

Figure 6.5 "European drugstore"
Credit: Solène Marié

6.3.2 Cultural networks, between formal and informal dynamics

The Brazil-Uruguay borderlands are spaces at the edge, in low density areas, with a historical coexistence of the State with a series of other actors who initiate processes which remain outside of the latter's control (AMILHAT SZARY, 2010). As highlighted by Ricardo Almeida, oversight is rich and brings freedom[49] (Figure 6.6).

Figure 6.6 Customs on the bridge linking Quaraí to Artigas
Credit: Solène Marié

Cultural projects in the Brazil-Uruguay borderlands take place not only in a spatial in-between but also in an institutional in-between which sometimes brings forth a legal one: prohibitively complex rules and regulations lead most actors to bypass them, think around them or skip them by obtaining support from strategic individuals.

Within the context of the France-Germany borderlands, Frédéric Duvinage[50] insists on the importance of informal processes in cross-border cooperation in general:

In the cultural field? It is the informal that works. [...] Things happen [...] when you meet people ... it's not in formal meetings with minutes and all that. [...] In fact, formalism [...] may just be the symptom of "we don't want to cooperate". Because with formalism you can always find a problem [...] in order not to do the project. In fact, people who want to do projects, they always find reasons for doing projects. And people who don't want to, they always find reasons not to.

6.3.3 Cultural ecosystems in the borderlands vs cross-border cultural projects

In their 2012 study for the French Ministry of Culture on the creation of European hubs of artistic production, Autissier and Deniau (2013a) highlight a tendency towards collaboration between cultural institutions which appears more as a result of public administration's leadership towards cooperation for management reasons, than based on cultural actors' actual desire to collaborate.

Clara Nieden[51] points out that all types of cooperation projects exist, from the cultural actor-led collaboration between Le Maillon theatre in Strasbourg and the Kulturbüro in Offenburg to the Museums-PASS card jointly giving access to cultural institutions in France, Germany and Switzerland, initiated by public administration. However, projects function better, according to her, when initiated by cultural actors.

This tendency is also observed in the Brazil-Uruguay borderlands. The positive links with Brasília mentioned by cultural actors in Santana do Livramento revolved around Culture Minister Juca Ferreira's visits to the border conurbation in 2010 and 2015 and in Jaguarão around the funds received through the PAC Cidades Históricas programme, which was a federal government collaboration with Brazilian IPHAN, with funds redistributed by the ministries of culture, education and tourism. Though this may be counter-intuitive, sectorial collaboration appears to bring more fluid cooperation processes and more effective results than general programmes designed by the Federal Government based exclusively on spatial criteria, even though they may be designed specifically for the borderlands.

6.3.4 Cultural ecosystems in the borderlands: at the centre of the edge

Autissier and Deniau (2013b, p. 102) highlight the fact that, based on the specificity of social capital as the only one which remains fixed, "the spatial proximity of protagonists, of interactions and of exchanges, seems to build trust based on the existence of a local identity and a joint tradition" (Figure 6.7).

At the same time, our study of the cultural networks in the Brazil-Uruguay borderlands demonstrated the significance of two dialectic processes in which the *outside* contributes to shaping the *inside*. Firstly, the outsider's perception of particularities of the borderlands can raise awareness of them locally.[52]

Cultural ecosystems in borderlands 123

Figure 6.7 Juxtaposed Uruguayan and Brazilian motorbikes
Credit: Solène Marié

Also, a significant number of local actors leave their native border city permanently or temporarily before coming back, and this process creates an engagement with the *inside*. This engagement can take the form of local engagement upon returning to the city or of an engagement at a distance within networks.

This type of network, whether formalised or not, has the advantage of presenting the ability to combine a sectorial dynamic with a spatial one: that of cultural action with that of the borderlands. According to Perrin (2013, p. 73), networks' "ability to navigate between project dynamics and institutional approach can enable them to bring an essential contribution to the renewal of public action."

Based on the confrontation of this theoretical work on cultural cross-border networks in the European context with the observations and analyses made in the context of the Brazil-Uruguay borderlands, the following typology appears. It integrates a number of informal dynamics which were seen as playing a fundamental role in the Brazil-Uruguay borderlands but also in the France-Germany borderlands and sees the functioning of cultural systems as based on three pillars: people, practices and places (Figure 6.8).

Three types of cultural ecosystems in borderlands emerge based on the predominance of two pillars: (1) cultural network predominance (based on the prevalence of the pillars of people and practices), (2) activism predominance (based on the prevalence of the pillars of people and places) and (3) territorial

124 Cultural ecosystems in borderlands

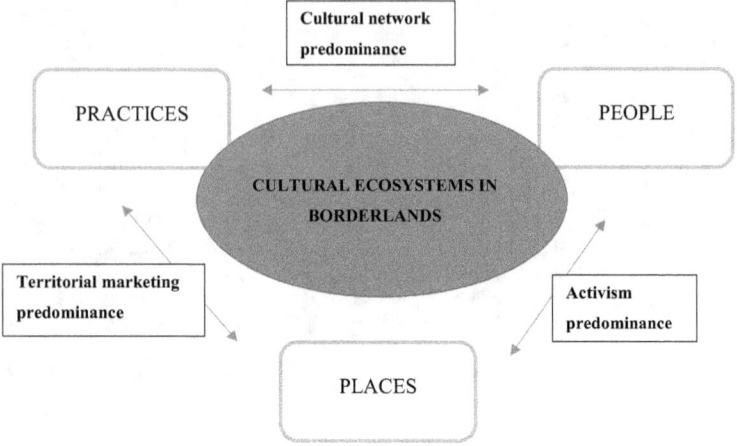

Figure 6.8 Pillars and types of cultural ecosystems in borderlands
Credit: Solène Marié

marketing predominance (based on the prevalence of the pillars of practices and places).

Whilst the cases encountered in the Brazil-Uruguay borderlands demonstrate a strong anchoring in the "people" pillar, those encountered in the France-Germany borderlands show their strong connection with "practices" in their cultural and institutional aspects. Thus, cases encountered in the former tend to come to life either through activism or through cultural networks (the two types connected to the pillar of people). In the latter, there is a predominance of cultural networks and territorial marketing (the two types connected to the pillar of practices). The analysis and model put forward in this thesis suggest that steady development of cultural ecosystems in borderlands is found by seeking balance between the three pillars and, thus, by aiming for the development of that which is weaker.

Notes

1 The most significant example would be the International Border Cinema Festival *[Festival Internacional de Cinema da Fronteira]* in Bagé and Pelotas.
2 Which can be translated to English as "Cultural borders movement". The original name will be maintained in the text.
3 Field notes from fieldwork conducted in the Brazil-Uruguay borderlands in July and September 2018.
4 Interview with Ricardo Almeida, project manager in the sectors of ICT and cultural integration. Conducted by the author by telephone, 10/09/2018.
5 *"Pensar o latino americano a partir da fronteira"*. Source: Interview with Ricardo Almeida conducted by the author. Op. cit.

Cultural ecosystems in borderlands 125

6 Corredores de integração cultural.
7 Interview with Ricardo Almeida. Op. cit.
8 *Festival Binacional de Enogastronomia e Produtos do Pampa.*
9 *Palácio Piratini:* governmental building of the Rio Grande do Sul state, situated in Porto Alegre.
10 Governor of the Rio Grande do Sul state from 2011 to 2015, from the Workers' Party (PT).
11 Interview with Jussara Dutra, ex-Chef of the Piratini Palace restaurant, creator and curator of the Binational Festival of Oeno-gastronomy. Conduted by the author in Santana do Livramento, 19/09/2018.
12 *Intendencia de Rivera.*
13 Interview with Jussara Dutra. Op. cit.
14 *Feira Binacional do Livro.*
15 *Carta da fronteira.*
16 In Uruguay, José Alberto "Pepe" Mujica Cordano (better known and hereafter referred to as Pepe Mujica), president from 2010 to 2015. In Brazil, Luiz Inácio Lula da Silva (better known and hereafter referred to as Lula), president from 2003 to 2011.
17 *Protocolo de Intenções Culturais.*
18 In Uruguay, Pepe Mujica. In Brazil, Dilma Rousseff.
19 Ana Lélia Benincá Beltrame.
20 Eliana da Costa.
21 Interview with Artur Montanari, joint owner of the Marco Zero bookshop and creator of the Santana do Livramento-Rivera Binational Book Fair. Conducted by the author in Santana do Livramento, 22/09/2018.
22 Interview with Artur Montanari. Op. cit.
23 Interview with Eduardo Palermo. Op. cit.
24 Interview with Artur Montanari. Op. cit.
25 Field notes from observation conducted by the author at an event bringing together visual artists from Santana do Livramento and Rivera, organized by the *Curadoria de Artes Visuais. Museo Departamental de Artes Plásticas*, Rivera, 18/09/2018.
26 Interview with Dionéia Macedo. Op. cit.
27 Interview with Mangela Britos. Op. cit.
28 Written communication from Artur Montanari.
29 The interviews were conducted by the author in 2018.
30 *Partido dos Trabalhadores.*
31 The choice of the city of Jaguarão to represent the municipal level here is based on fieldwork which pointed to a significant phenomenon of political convergence which was seized as an opportunity for the leading of projects.
32 From 2015, Mayor Claudio Martins was involved in legal processes.
33 On the 12th of May 2015, Dilma Rousseff left power in the context of an impeachment procedure.
34 Instituto do Patrimônio Histórico e Artístico do Estado.
35 Ana Lúcia de Oliveira.
36 Interview with Alan Dutra de Melo, Professor of Cultural Policy and Production at UNIPAMPA, previously a member of Jaguarão city council's cultural department. Conducted by the author in Jaguarão, 10/09/2018.
37 Interview with Adriana Ança, Architect and member of Jaguarão's urban planning department. Conducted by the author in Jaguarão, 13/09/2018.
38 Interview with Jussara Dutra. Op. cit.
39 Interview with Jussara Dutra. Op. cit.
40 Santana do Livramento in the case of Ricardo Almeida; the borderlands between Brazil and Argentina in the case of Jussara Dutra.
41 Interview with Jussara Dutra. Op. cit.
42 Interview with Margot Bernardi, project officer at IBA Basel. Conducted by the author by telephone, 05/06/2019.

43 The only exception being the *Jaguararte* festival in Jaguarão.
44 Interview with Frédérique Chabaud, Advisor on Culture, Youth, Education, Media and Sport for The Greens/European Free Alliance, European Parliament. Conducted by the author by telephone, 28/05/2019.
45 Interview with Frédérique Chabaud. Op. cit.
46 Interview with Anne Poidevin, literature officer at DRAC Grand Est, previously international cultural policy officer at city and eurometropolis of Strasbourg. Conducted by the author by telephone, 30/08/2019.
47 Interview with Anne Poidevin. Op. cit.
48 Field notes from an interview with Aurélie Reveillaud, Project manager at Creative Europe French office, previously a member of the *Perspectives* festival team. Conducted by the author at Le Shadok, Strasbourg, 10/05/2019.
49 Interview with Ricardo Almeida. Op. cit.
50 Interview with Frédéric Duvinage, Director of the Basel trinational eurodistrict. Conducted by the author by telephone, 08/07/2019.
51 Interview with Clara Nieden, cross-border and European cooperation project manager at DRAC Grand Est. Conducted by the author in Le Shadok, Strasbourg, 09/05/2019.
52 Interview with Dionéia de Macedo. Op. cit.

References

ALMEIDA, R.; DORFMAN, A. Fronteiras Culturais/Fronteras Culturales: um processo de autonomias e de convergências. **Anuário Unbral das Fronteiras Brasileiras**, v. 3, pp. 135–152, 2017.

AMILHAT SZARY, A. Frontières et intégration régionale en Amérique Latine: sur la piste du chaînon manquant. In: FLAESCH-MOUGIN, C.; LEBULLENGER, J. [eds]. **Regards croisés sur les intégrations régionales Europe/Amériques**. Editions Bruylant, collection Rencontres Européennes, 2010, pp. 307–341.

AUTISSIER, Anne-Marie. **L'alternative européenne des festivals transnationaux**: Les Boréales et Reims Scènes d'Europe. Working paper presented at Atelier de recherche de l'EFRP, Université de Strasbourg, Centre de sociologie européenne, 2011.

AUTISSIER, Anne-Marie; DENIAU, Marie. **Etude prospective sur la mise en place de pôles européens de production artistique**. Observatoire des Politiques Culturelles/Ministère de la Culture et de la Communication, 2013a.

AUTISSIER, Anne-Marie; DENIAU, Marie. Synthèse d'Etude. Tisser l'Europe culturelle à partir des territoires. Dynamiques de regroupement et initiatives européennes. **L'Observatoire Plus**. n. 43, pp. 102–106, 2013b.

BENTO, Fábio Régio. O papel das cidades gêmeas de fronteira na integração regional sul-americana. **Revista Conjuntura Austral**. v. 6, n. 27-28, pp. 50–53, dez. 2014–mar. 2015.

CLEMENTE, Isabel. La Región De Frontera Uruguay-Brasil y La Relación Binacional: Pasado y Perspectivas. **Revista Uruguaya de Ciencia Política**, v. 19, n. 1, pp. 165–184, 2010.

JESUS, Diego Santos Vieira de. A arte do encontro: a paradiplomacia e a internacionalização das cidades criativas. **Revista de Sociologia e Política**, v. 25, n. 61, pp. 51–76, 2017.

MERCHER, L.; BERNARDO, G.; SILVA, E. **South American Cities and Frontiers: An analysis of regional integration from Mercocities Network**. Working paper presented at the International Studies Association annual convention, San Francisco, April 2018.

MORAES, Margarete. Caminhadas além das fronteiras. In: MARTINS, Maria Helena [org]. **Fronteiras Culturais. Brasil – Uruguai – Argentina**. Cotia: Ateliê Editorial, 2002.

PERRIN, T. La gouvernance culturelle dans les eurorégions: enjeux et dynamiques. **Eurolimes. Journal of the Institute for Euroregional Studies Oradea-Debrecen**, v. 16, pp. 63–78, 2013.

PERRIN, T. Creative regions on a European cross-border scale: Policy issues and development perspectives. **European Planning Studies**, v. 23, n. 12, pp. 2423–2437 2015.

SAEZ, Guy. Gouvernance culturelle territoriale: les acteurs. In: SAEZ, Guy [dir]. **Institutions et vie culturelles**. Paris: La Documentation française, 2004.

ZAMORANO, Mariano Martín; MORATÓ, Arturo Rodríguez. The cultural paradiplomacy of Barcelona since the 1980s: understanding transformations in local cultural paradiplomacy. **International Journal of Cultural Policy**, v. 21, n. 5, pp. 554–576, 2014.

7 Conclusion

The aim of this book was to provide a contribution to the analysis of processes occurring in borderlands, specifically those around cultural production and policy. It stemmed from the observation of a pattern linked to the existence, in some borderlands, of networks of cultural action which cross an international land border.

It was structured around the aim of understanding the processes and networks that sustain this cultural action, looking at the relative contribution of processes led by institutions, cultural agents and the civil society as well as of formal and informal practices. In order to understand how these processes translate across different cross-border spaces, it was based on two cases: that of the Brazil-Uruguay borderlands and of the France-Germany borderlands.

The incipient nature of research on Brazilian borderlands, the weak representation of South American borderlands in worldwide literature on the subject as well as the few existing cross-regional perspectives on borderland processes justified fully this choice of cases.

Both cases present similar characteristics: current observable cross-border cultural processes and networks, and historical similarities in terms of shifting of the borderline, alternating national allegiances, movements of populations as well as a role as a buffer space between two regional powers.

An inductive, case-centred, asymmetrical study of the two cases was set up, aiming to explore each case fully and individually in its own historical and cultural context before proceeding to the creation of data-driven categories of analysis. More emphasis was placed upon the first case, the Brazil-Uruguay borderlands, in order to offer a contribution to the literature on Southern borders, produced in the South. The second case, the France-Germany borderlands, was approached as a counterpoint to the first one in order to bring depth and contrast to the analysis. The approach to literature was also asymmetrical as a response to the difference in quantity of literature on the subject produced in Europe compared to South America, which could result in a Eurocentric bias in the approach to the first case. This approach also aimed to compensate the difference in quantity and quality of primary data available on the two cases, requiring more in-depth interviews in the first case.

Conclusion 129

Furthermore, though an effort was made to elaborate this research from the borderlands as a whole through fieldwork that attempted to enter different networks and gather varied viewpoints, it was constructed based on the author's much deeper knowledge of the Brazilian and French contexts than of the Uruguayan and German ones. Therefore, descriptions and analysis of processes and actors are more rooted in the former two contexts.

Chapter 2 presented the various existing concepts and debates around the main two themes of this thesis: borders and culture. It demonstrated how various conceptions of the notion of border coexist within scholarship on the subject in perspectives that are often seen as contradictory, though they can actually be considered various aspects of a multifaceted object. There is a tendency in literature to adopt a vision of borders that relates more to one of the conceptions (borders as lines, as zones, as relational spaces or as institutions) or to look at them one at a time. It was argued that borderlands combine all these dimensions, which are not mutually exclusive and tend to alternate depending on practices, time and actors involved. Subsequently, the main possible ways of envisioning cultural issues in borderlands were presented in order to build the theoretical basis of the book and justify the options made in terms of how to approach them. Finally, the chapter presented the development of border scholarship, its current characteristics and a number of widely disseminated models for the study of cultural and integration issues in borderlands. Based on this analysis, a number of choices were made in terms of concepts and vocabulary used in the research.

In Chapter 3, the analytical model for the study was developed, taking into account a number of issues and difficulties with the analysis of both the topics of borders and of culture within the discipline of international relations (IR). An approach focusing on everyday international relations was set up, envisaging borderlands as spaces where international relations take place, albeit on a different scale, involving other actors and according to different processes from those relating to international relations studied through the interactions between central governments or global actors. Based on a description of the development of cultural discussions within the field of IR and of a number of limits present in IR scholarship regarding the study of cultural issues, an operationalised outlook on the notion of culture was designed. Three categories of observables were defined: cultural networks, cultural actions (policies and projects) and topography of culture. A multi-sited ethnographic approach was set up with the aim of identifying practices and relationships through fieldwork, based on connections and associations between human and institutional relationships. Within both borderlands, the choice was made to focus the analysis on border urban centres: Jaguarão-Rio Branco and Santana do Livramento-Rivera in the Brazil-Uruguay borderlands and Strasbourg-Kehl and Saint-Louis-Weil am Rhein-Basel in the France Germany borderlands. In both cases, the first urban centre is composed of two discontinuous municipalities including a large city and a small town whilst the second one is composed of a continuous urban centre.

Chapters 4 and 5 presented two cases: the Brazil-Uruguay borderlands and the France-Germany borderlands. They started with presentations of the historical, geographic, demographic and cultural context of both cases. The presentation of different aspects of shared culture which can be encountered in these borderlands, though not intending to be exhaustive, served to demonstrate the existence of some elements of cultural convergence, especially in urban areas. They demonstrated how these borderlands are profoundly rooted in processes and characteristics which are influenced by the presence of the borderline and which have affected their constitution as social spaces. Subsequently and for each of the cases, the processes and actors involved in the development of cross-border cultural networks were described. Starting with the contribution *to cultural governance in the borderlands* of institutional actors at various levels of government, it went on to analyse the contribution of processes of an activist nature through the study of their spatial and social aspects as well as of the processes involved.

In Chapter 6, the confrontation between the two cases shed light on three common aspects between the processes at work: the importance of the leadership of projects, the influence of windows of opportunity and the advantages of projects involving a tangible, marketable and perennial product. Regarding the nature of cultural ecosystems in borderlands, the following characteristics were described: a confronting logic of presence and absence of the border, an influence of the marginality of those spaces on their functioning as systems, a combination of formal and informal dynamics at play and the profoundly cultural nature of the networks which enable the creation of long-lasting initiatives. Finally, a three-dimensional typology was elaborated for the analysis of the building blocks and characteristics of these systems.

Index

Note: **Bold** page numbers refer to tables; *italic* page numbers refer to figures and page numbers followed by "n" denote endnotes.

activism 110, 116, 123, 124
actors 101, 102, 106, 110–114, 117, 118, 122
Ad Hoc Group on Borderland Integration (GAHIF) 58
Agreement on the Residence of Nationals of Mercosul Member States and from Bolivia and Chile 78
Almeida, Ricardo 106, 116, 121
Alsacian dialects 98
Andrade, Mário de 70
Anzaldúa, Gloria 11; *Borderlands/La Frontera. The New Mestiza* 11
Argentina-Brazil border *6–7*, 82n5
article 21, Brazilian constitution (1988) 69–70
Artigas 41, 44, 53
Artigas, José 43, 44, 51
artistic production 20, 33, 122
artists 4, 54, 55, 68, 69, 101, 106, 111, 120

Banda Oriental 44
Barón of Mauá International Bridge 49, *49*, 59, 69
Basel/Basel Trinational 91, 95, 96–98, 103n3, 118
Binational Book Fair 64, 109, 112
Binational Festival of Oeno-gastronomy 108, *109*, 111, 114, 118, 119
Board of International Relations (DRI) 68, 118
Border Committees of twin cities 76–78, 111
Border Dialogue 69
Border Integration Workgroup (UTIF) 79

borderlanders 10–13, 22, 29, 42, 49, 51, 61, 76
Borderland Integration Zone 61, 78
borderland(s) 1, 4; concept of 10–12; cooperation 58, 64, 76, 120; cultural issues in 19–21; definition of 30–31, 37; development of 99; dynamics 2, 29; integration 61, 76–78, 110; size and shape of 31
Borderlands/La Frontera. The New Mestiza (Anzaldúa) 11
border(s) 1, *17*; and border spaces as institutions 15–17, **17**; culture 105, 129; definition 6; interdependent 24; as limits 8–10, **9**, 17, 18; as relational spaces 13–15, 17, 18; representation of 6; scholarship 21, 23, 36, 129; strip 13, 95; studies 21, 22; trends and issues 22–24; as zones 10–13, 18
Border Schools project 81
Border Strip Development and Integration Plans 65
boundaries 18
Brasília 62, 69, 122
Brazil 2, 4, 13, 36, 40, 42, 44, 46, 49, 50, 51, 54, 57–61, 64, 66, 68–70, 75, 77, 106
Brazilian Border Strip 76, 78
Brazilian Cooperation Agency (ABC) 81, 82
Brazilian Federal programmes 63
Brazilian IPHAN 122
Brazilian Ministry of Education 81
Brazilian Ministry of Foreign Affairs (MRE) 66, 68, 82, 118

132 Index

Brazilian National Institute of Historic and Artistic Heritage (IPHAN) 59, 69
Brazil-Uruguay borderlands 2–4, 7, 36–37, 40–82, 128–130; cultural and linguistic features 53–55; cultural governance (*see* cultural governance in Brazil-Uruguay borderlands); cultural networks in 106, 114–119, 122–124; demographics 51–52; economic activity and networks 49–51; geographical contextualisation 40, 42; historical contextualisation 42–46, *44*; shifts in political and territorial affiliation 45, *45*; tangibility and perennial festivals 119, 130; urbanisation 46–49, *48*; *see also* cultural ecosystems
Buenos Aires 53, 54

Canning, George 42
Cardoso, Fernando Henrique 66
Cartilha do Programa de Desenvolvimento da Faixa de Fronteira (PDFF) 64, 65, 69, 76, 78, 81
Casa de Cultura 109
Chuí-Chuy *52*
Cisplatine Province 44
citizenship 51, 52, 76, 77
civil society 1, 14, 33, 76, 77, 110, 116, 128
Committee for the Internationalisation of Brazilian Culture 68
conflict 8, 15, 18, 19, 35, 37, 44, 46, 50, 51, 55, 70, 109
Consejo de Educación Técnico Profesional-Universidad del Trabajo del Uruguay (CETP-UTU) 81, 82
consulate 78, 109, 111–112
continuous urban centre 96, *97*
conurbation 47, 48, *48, 52,* 77, 79, 105, 108, 116
Convention on the Protection and Promotion of the Diversity of Cultural Expressions (2005) 33
Council of Europe 101
creative cities 75, 106
Creative Europe programme 100
cross-border: cooperation 30, 99, 102, 121; culture 1, 3; integration 12–13, 22, 30, 99, 120; processes 2, 3; regions 16; spaces 1, 3, 16
cross-regional analysis 2, 3
cultural ecosystems 3, 105–124, 130; actors 110–114; *vs.* cross-border cultural projects 122; cultural actions 106–109; formal and informal dynamics 121–122; pillars and types of 122–124, *124*; presence and absence of border 120; spatial, institutional and social (re)compositions 114–119; topography 105–106
cultural governance in Brazil-Uruguay borderlands 55–63, 64–66, 68–72, 74–79, 81–82; Federal State59–66, 68–70; Mercosul 56–59; municipalities 75–79, 81–82; Rio Grande do Sul state 69–72, 74–75
cultural networks 1, 99, 105, 129; cross-border 110, 113; formal and informal dynamics 121–122
cultural policy 1, 3, 4, 57, 70, 72, 75, 99; conception of 35; definitions of 19–21, **20**
cultural production 1, 105, 106, 128; in borderlands 28–37, 75; cross-border 3
Culture 2000 100
culture(al): actions 20–21, 36, 72, 101–102, 106–107, 108–110, 123, 128, 129; anachronistic concept of 34; capital 106; convergence 55, 130; cooperation 66, **67**; diplomacy 33–34, 57, 66, 68; diversity 57, 66; economy 57; events 111; heritage 33; identities 1, 36; industries 119; institutions 4, 106, 122; integration 54, 57, 71, 106–107; internationalism 32; issues 19–21, 71, 112; practices 106; projects 1, 56, 75, 100, 101, **116, 117,** 117, 118, 119, 121; transfers 32; turn 32

democracy 24
Dutra, Jussara 108, 114, 116, 118

economy(ic): activity 49–51, 95; development 60; exchange 49; growth 50
educational cooperation 66, **67**
Education Law (1877) 53
EU Cohesion Policy 100
EU Member-States 100
EU programmes 100, 118, 119
European Commission 101
European Constitution project 98
European immigration 51
European Territorial Cooperation 100, 101
European Union (EU) 4, 58, 99–103

Federal Constitution (1934) 59
Federal Government 122; Brazilian Federal Government 64
federal instruments **63**
Federal University of Pelotas 113–114
Ferreira, Juca 122
foreign policy 33, 34, 57, 68, 70
formal cooperation 1, 3
France 13
France-Germany borderlands 2–4, 11, 13, 36–37, 91–103, 128–130; cultural governance 99–103; cultural networks in 114–119, 124; demographic, economic and cultural contextualisation 95–96, *96*, 98–99, *99*; geographical contextualisation 91–93, *91–93*; historical contextualisation 93–95, **94**; tangibility and perennial festivals 119; *see also* cultural ecosystems
Franco-Prussian War 94
Frankfurt Treaty (1871) 94
free trade 13
French Ministry of Culture 122
Fronteras Culturales/Fronteiras Culturais movement 106–107, **107**, *108*, 116, 118
frontiers 8, 14, 21
Fund for the Structural Convergence and Strengthening of the Institutional Structure (FOCEM) 58
funding 65, 66, 69, 100–102, 108, 109, 119

gaúcha identity 71
Geertz, Clifford 19
Genro, Tarso 108, 118
geopolitics 10, 21
Grand Est region 93, 95, *96*, 102
Growth Acceleration Programme (PAC) for Historical Cities 68–69, 119, 122
Guarani indigenous communities 82n5

hard power 32–33, 57
Huningue 91, 96, 103n5
hybrid space/hybrid culture/hybridity 2, 12, 18, 37

IBA Basel 118
informal cooperation 1, 3
Institute of Historic and Artistic Heritage of the Rio Grande do Sul State (IPHAE) 113, 114
institutionalisation 2, 3, 24, 71, 75–77, 78

institutional structure 71, 78, 95, 101–102
Instituto Federal Sul-Riograndense (IFSul) 81
interdependence 14, 50, 75, 106
interdisciplinarity 21–22, 28, 36
internal/external dichotomy 29–30
International Bookfair 118
international culture: issues 32; relations 33, 34
internationalisation 75
International Park 109
international relations (IR) 1, 4, 10, 12, 22; borders in 29; study of everyday 29, 129; *see also* cultural study and IR
Interreg programme 99, 101, 118

Jaguarão Cultural Department 65
Jaguarão Cultural Municipal Council 65
Jaguarão-Rio Branco 47, *47,* 49, *49–50,* 59, 105, 111, 129
Jaguar Project 114
Jesuit Mission settlements 82n5
Journal of Borderlands Studies 23

Kaleidoscope 100
Kehl-Strasbourg *see* Strasbourg-Kehl

Latin America 23, 71, 110
Lavaleja, Juan Antonio 44
leadership 116–117, 130
League of Nations 95
Lei Rouanet tax incentive 108
Le Maillon theatre 122
Lula da Silva, Luiz Inácio 62, 64, 66

Maastricht Treaty (1992) 100
Maginot line 94
Marco Zero bookshop 109
marketing documents *108,* 120
Martins, Claudio 125n32
MEDIA Mundus Programme 100
Meeting of Ministers of Culture (RMC) 56
Memorandum of Understanding 56
Mercocities Network 69, 79, **80–81**
Mercosur 2, 56–59, 78, 79, 110
Mercosur Audiovisual Programme 57
Mercosur Cultural 56, 59
Mercosur Cultural Fund 57
Mercosur Cultural Information System (SICSUR) 56
Mercosur Cultural Integration Protocol 56
Mercosur Cultural Parliament (PARCUM) 56

Index

Mercosur Specialized Meeting on Culture 56
Ministério da Educação (MEC) 82
Ministry of Culture (MinC) 66, 68, 71, 118
Ministry of Foreign Affairs' Federative Relations Advisory Board 70
Ministry of National Integration 77, 78, 81
Montevideo 53
MRE Cultural Department 66
Mujica, José 61, 118
multidisciplinary orientation 23, 36
multi-sited ethnography 105, 129; as everyday IR tool 36–37
municipalities 75–82, 83n47, 105
Museums-PASS 122
musical networks 54

National Cultural System 70
National Defence Council (CDN) 59
National Institute of Historic and Artistic Heritage (IPHAN) 113
nationality 9
National Regional Development Policy 65
National Security Strip 59
National Superior Security Council 59
nation state 29
networks 4, 31, 36, 46, 50, 76, 95; *see also* cultural networks; musical networks
New Agenda for Borderland Cooperation and Development between Brazil and Uruguay 61, 77
Nye, Joseph 32

Oriental Republic of Uruguay 44

Pampa 108
paradiplomatic activity 69–72, **72–74,** 106
Peace of Westphalia (1648) 9
Permanent Commission for the Development of the Border Strip 64
political convergence 113–114
porosity 2, 37
Portuguese language 53
Portunhol/Portuñol 53–54
president 64, 66, 113, 118
producers 4, 100, 106
Programa de Desenvolvimento da Faixa de Fronteira (PPDF) 79, 81, 82
protectionist policies 51
public policy 2, 64, 65, 70–71, 72, 75, 77

regional development 60, 77, 81, 110
regionalisation 46, 53, 110
Relais Culture Europe 101
Rio Branco 43, 44, 49, 59
Rio Branco-Jaguarão *see* Jaguarão-Rio Branco
Rio de la Plata 40, 43, 44, 54
Rio Grande do Sul 50, 51, 69–72, **72–74,** 74–75, 108, 118
Rivera-Santana do Livramento *see* Santana do Livramento-Rivera

Saarland 91, 95
Saint Louis-Weil am Rhein-Basel 96–99, *97,* 105, 129
saladeros 50
salted meat production 50, 51
San Ildefonso Treaty (1777) 43
Santana do Livramento-Rivera 46–47, *47, 48, 50,* 51, 58, *58,* 59, 78, 105–108, 110–112, 114, 116, 118, 119, 122, 129
Santos, Osmar 55
Schlee, Aldyr Garcia 54
shared culture 54, 55, 130
Siegfried line 94
slavery 50, 52
smuggling 50
social capital 122
social identity 3, 11
Sociology of Public Action 20
soft power 32, 33, 57
South America 13, 43, 79
South American borders/borderlands 4, 24, 43, 110, 128
Southern Common Market *see* Mercosur
sovereign States 9, 22
sovereignty 9, 15, 29, 30, 34
Special Borderlander Documents 78
Special Borderlander ID 78
Specialized Meeting of Mercosur Cinematographic and Audiovisual Authorities (RECAM) 57
Special Secretariat for International Affairs (SEAI) 71
Standard German 98
State-centric perspectives 29–30, 31
Strasbourg-Kehl 96, *97,* 105, 129
Swabian dialects 98
Swiss German 98
Szary, Amilhat 8, 9, 37, 43, 110, 121

Index 135

territorial boundaries 28
territorialisation 13–14
territorial marketing 123, 124
territorial principle 15
territorial socialisation 16, 24n6
Thirty Years' War 94
tourism 119
transition zones 11, 14, 37
translation 34, 43, 53–54, 128
Treaty of Asunción (1991) 56, 57
Treaty of Limits (1851) 44
twin cities 47, 103n4, 105, 106

United Nations Development Programme (UNDP) 81, 82
United Nations Educational, Scientific and Cultural Organization (UNESCO) 19, 21, 33, 35
universities 113–114
university professors 4, 69, 82
urban centres 96, 98, 129–130
urbanisation 2, 31, *48*

Uruguay 13, 41–44, 52–54, 59
Uruguayan Portuguese Dialects (DPU) 54
US-Mexico borderlands 23
uti possidetis de facto/uti possidetis juris principle 43, 44

Varela, José Pedro 53
Vargas, Getúlio 51, 70
Vauban, Sébastien Le Prestre de 93
Versailles Treaty (1920) 94
visual arts 55

Walker, R.B.J. 29, 35
Warndt Forest 95
Weil am Rhein-Saint Louis-Basel *see* Saint Louis-Weil am Rhein-Basel
Workers' Party (PT) 113
Working Group for Border Integration within the Mercocities Network 113
World War I 94, 95
World War II 93, 94, 95

Taylor & Francis eBooks

www.taylorfrancis.com

A single destination for eBooks from Taylor & Francis with increased functionality and an improved user experience to meet the needs of our customers.

90,000+ eBooks of award-winning academic content in Humanities, Social Science, Science, Technology, Engineering, and Medical written by a global network of editors and authors.

TAYLOR & FRANCIS EBOOKS OFFERS:

- A streamlined experience for our library customers
- A single point of discovery for all of our eBook content
- Improved search and discovery of content at both book and chapter level

REQUEST A FREE TRIAL
support@taylorfrancis.com

For Product Safety Concerns and Information please contact our EU representative GPSR@taylorandfrancis.com
Taylor & Francis Verlag GmbH, Kaufingerstraße 24, 80331 München, Germany

www.ingramcontent.com/pod-product-compliance
Lightning Source LLC
Chambersburg PA
CBHW051749230426
43670CB00012B/2219